CAMBRIDGE LIBRARY COLLECTION

Books of enduring scholarly value

Travel and Exploration

The history of travel writing dates back to the Bible, Caesar, the Vikings and the Crusaders, and its many themes include war, trade, science and recreation. Explorers from Columbus to Cook charted lands not previously visited by Western travellers, and were followed by merchants, missionaries, and colonists, who wrote accounts of their experiences. The development of steam power in the nineteenth century provided opportunities for increasing numbers of 'ordinary' people to travel further, more economically, and more safely, and resulted in great enthusiasm for travel writing among the reading public. Works included in this series range from first-hand descriptions of previously unrecorded places, to literary accounts of the strange habits of foreigners, to examples of the burgeoning numbers of guidebooks produced to satisfy the needs of a new kind of traveller - the tourist.

Reports on the Discovery of Peru

The publications of the Hakluyt Society (founded in 1846) made available edited (and sometimes translated) early accounts of exploration. The first series, which ran from 1847 to 1899, consists of 100 books containing published or previously unpublished works by authors from Christopher Columbus to Sir Francis Drake, and covering voyages to the New World, to China and Japan, to Russia and to Africa and India. This volume, published in 1872, contains four eye-witness accounts of the Spanish conquest of Peru, translated and edited by Clements R. Markham, the Honorary Secretary of the Society from 1858 to 1887, and then its President for twenty years. The authors, who include Francisco Pizarro's secretary and his brother Hernando, recount the events leading to the downfall of the Inca empire. The final document is a notary's account of the distribution of the gold and silver – the legendary 'one room full of gold and two rooms full of silver' – which the Incas paid to the Spaniards in a vain attempt to save the life of their ruler, Atahualpa.

Cambridge University Press has long been a pioneer in the reissuing of out-of-print titles from its own backlist, producing digital reprints of books that are still sought after by scholars and students but could not be reprinted economically using traditional technology. The Cambridge Library Collection extends this activity to a wider range of books which are still of importance to researchers and professionals, either for the source material they contain, or as landmarks in the history of their academic discipline.

Drawing from the world-renowned collections in the Cambridge University Library, and guided by the advice of experts in each subject area, Cambridge University Press is using state-of-the-art scanning machines in its own Printing House to capture the content of each book selected for inclusion. The files are processed to give a consistently clear, crisp image, and the books finished to the high quality standard for which the Press is recognised around the world. The latest print-on-demand technology ensures that the books will remain available indefinitely, and that orders for single or multiple copies can quickly be supplied.

The Cambridge Library Collection will bring back to life books of enduring scholarly value (including out-of-copyright works originally issued by other publishers) across a wide range of disciplines in the humanities and social sciences and in science and technology.

Reports on the Discovery of Peru

EDITED BY CLEMENTS R. MARKHAM

CAMBRIDGE UNIVERSITY PRESS

Cambridge, New York, Melbourne, Madrid, Cape Town, Singapore,
São Paolo, Delhi, Dubai, Tokyo, Mexico City

Published in the United States of America by Cambridge University Press, New York

www.cambridge.org
Information on this title: www.cambridge.org/9781108010610

This edition first published 1872
This digitally printed version 2010

ISBN 978-1-108-01061-0 Paperback

WORKS ISSUED BY

The Hakluyt Society.

REPORTS

ON THE DISCOVERY OF PERU.

M.DCCC.LXXII.

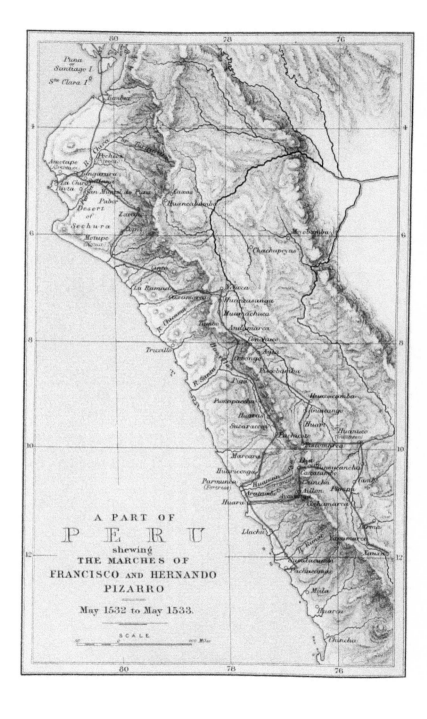

80   78   76

Puna or
Santiago I.
Sta Clara I.°

Tumbez

Amotape
(Abrojos)
Tangarara
La Chira
Paita   San Miguel de Piura
Pabor
Zaran
Motupe (Xayanca)
Desert of
Sechura

R. Chira
Pechico
(Copis)

Saxas
Huancabamba

Moyobamba

Chachapoyas

Xanco

La Ramada
Chicama
N. Chicama
Cazamarca
Tambo
Andamarca
Conchuco
Ayza

Xauca
Huamasanga
Huamachuca

Trucillo
R. Santa
Otonga
Piga
Pircobamba

Punapaccha
Huaras
Sucaracon
Huari
Pachacte
Huaracamba
Huancayo
Huanuco
(Palaces)

Marcara
Aztomarca
Huaricongo
Parmunca
(Fortress)
Huara
Aratambe
Uya
Huanaucancha
Cazatambo
Ayavarcu
Chincha
Ayllon
Pisapa
Pichamarca
Tambo

Llachu
Rimac
Xauxa
Yanamarca
Yanac
Sacalacuaxa
Pachacongo
Mala
Huarco
Chincha

A PART OF
P E R U
shewing
THE MARCHES OF
FRANCISCO AND HERNANDO
PIZARRO

May 1532 to May 1533.

SCALE
50   100 Miles

80   78   76

4   6   8   10   12

REPORTS

ON THE

DISCOVERY OF PERU.

I.

REPORT OF FRANCISCO DE XERES, SECRETARY TO FRANCISCO PIZARRO.

II.

REPORT OF MIGUEL DE ASTETE ON THE EXPEDITION
TO PACHACAMAC.

III.

LETTER OF HERNANDO PIZARRO TO THE ROYAL AUDIENCE OF
SANTO DOMINGO.

IV.

REPORT OF PEDRO SANCHO ON THE PARTITION OF THE
RANSOM OF ATAHUALLPA.

TRANSLATED AND EDITED,

With Notes and an Introduction,

BY

CLEMENTS R. MARKHAM, C.B.

LONDON:

PRINTED FOR THE HAKLUYT SOCIETY.

M.DCCC.LXXII.

COUNCIL

OF

THE HAKLUYT SOCIETY.

CONTENTS,

WITH THE

ITINERARIES OF FRANCISCO & HERNANDO PIZARRO.

viii

CONTENTS,

ITINERARY OF HERNANDO PIZARRO, IN THE REPORT OF
ASTETE.

b

INTRODUCTION.

FRANCISCO DE XERES, the Secretary of Pizarro, wrote his account of the early days of the conquest of Peru, on the spot, by order of his master. He sailed from San Lucar, with Pizarro, in January 1530, was with the conqueror in his voyage, in his march along the Peruvian coast and across the Andes, and was an eye-witness of the events at Cassamarca, down to the murder of the Ynca Atahuallpa. He returned to Seville on July 3rd, 1534, after an absence of four years and a half, with the first instalments of gold. His friends lived at Seville, and I gather from Argote de Molina[1] that he came of a respectable family settled at Ubeda; but nothing is known of himself personally, beyond what can be deduced from his narrative.

The narrative of Xeres appears to have been printed at Seville in 1534, the year of his return, but this first edition is extremely scarce. The second edition, which was very carelessly printed, appeared at Salamanca in 1547, and is also very rare. The

---

[1] *Nobleza de Andalusia* (Sevilla, 1588), p. 66. Argote de Molina gives the arms of the Xeres family. *Vert, in base waves of the sea azure and argent, on them a tower argent and fastened to it a boat with its oar or. On a bordure gules eight St. Andrew's crosses or.*

third, and best known Spanish edition, was published
at Madrid, in the collection of Don Andres Gonzalez
Barcia,[2] in 1749. The work was translated into
Italian by a native of Tudela, named Domingo de
Gaztelù, who was Secretary to Lope de Soria, Ambassador to Venice for Charles V, and published at
Venice in 1535. A second edition of the Italian
version was published at Venice, in the collection of
Ramusio,[3] in 1556. Purchas gives a very brief
notice of it, in his *Pilgrimes;*[4] and Ticknor mentions
the work in his history of Spanish literature.[5] It is
much quoted by Robertson, Prescott, and Helps, in
their accounts of the conquest of Peru. A careful
French version was published at Paris, by M. Ternaux Compans,[6] in his series of works on Spanish
America, in 1837; but no complete English translation has hitherto been made.

As the account of an intelligent and observant
eye-witness, the story told by Francisco de Xeres,
of the most stirring episode in the wonderful history
of Spanish conquests, is exceedingly interesting.
Some portions of the story, here and there, are told
in more detail by Herrera and other compilers, but,
in reading their versions, we miss the feeling that
the author was an actor in the deeds he narrates;

[2] "*Historiadores Primitivos de las Indias Occidentales,*" iii, p.
179. [3] *Ramusio,* iii, pp. 378-98.

[4] *Purchas, Pilgrimes,* iv, pp. 1491-94.

[5] *Ticknor,* i, p. 521.

[6] "*Voyages, relations et mémoires originaux pour servir à l'histoire
de la découverte de l'Amérique*" (Paris, 1837). H. Ternaux
Compans.

and thus, in Xeres, there is a freshness and reality which no other published account of the conquest can impart. Xeres himself relates the proceedings of the Governor Francisco Pizarro. But he has given much increased value to his work, by embodying in it the report by Miguel Astete, another eye-witness, of the expedition of Hernando Pizarro, to the famous temple of Pachacamac. This remarkable journey of Hernando in quest of gold, undertaken by a mere handful of men into the heart of an unknown land, is as attractive to the imagination as the incredible audacity of Francisco's enterprise. Xeres and Astete were both eye-witnesses, and their detailed narratives combine to record the incidents of two of the most surprising marches in the history of Spanish discovery.

The letter of Hernando Pizarro to the Royal Audience of Santo Domingo,[7] which follows the narrative of Xeres, was written when that ruthless conqueror was on his way to Spain, with the king's share of the spoils. It goes over exactly the same ground as the Reports of Xeres and Astete, it is peculiarly valuable as containing the observations of the man of highest rank in the expedition who could write, and the slight variations between the accounts of Xeres and Pizarro, in relating the same incidents, are particularly interesting. One very odious peculiarity of Hernando Pizarro was, that he habitually

---

[7] In the "*Historia General*" of Oviedo, cap. xv, lib. 43. Reprinted in the "*Vidas de Españoles célebres, por Don Manuel Josef Quintana*" (Paris, 1845), p. 180.

tortured the Indians when he wished to obtain information from them. Yet on the three occasions on which he mentions having applied the torture, in this letter, he was told lies. One would have thought that so acute an observer would have discovered that this was a very inefficient method of conducting the operations of an Intelligence Department. The fourth document in this volume is the Report of Pedro Sancho on the distribution of the ransom of Atahuallpa ;[8] in which he gives the amounts received by each of the conquerors.

Hernando Pizarro and Miguel de Astete give us the first account of the temple of Pachacamac on the Peruvian coast, which was afterwards described by Cieza de Leon and Garcilasso de la Vega, and the real significance of which is not fully understood, and has been a good deal exaggerated. The subject is one which may appropriately be discussed in an Introduction to the narratives of Hernando Pizarro and Astete ; and the following remarks will perhaps invest them with some additional interest.

The famous temple on the Pacific coast has usually been supposed to have been the only temple to the Supreme Being in Peru ; and it has even been suggested that, as such, it is older than the time of the Yncas, and that they adopted this worship from another people. Mr. Prescott[9] says that no temple

---

[8] From the inedited work of Francisco Lopez de Caravantes. It is reprinted in the "*Vidas de Españoles célèbres, por Don Manuel Josef Quintana*" (Paris, 1845), p. 185.

[9] *Prescott*, i, p. 85.

was raised to Pachacamac, the Creator of the World,
save one only which took its name from the Deity
Himself; that it existed before the country came
under the sway of the Yncas, and was a resort of
pilgrims from remote parts of the land; and that
these circumstances suggest the idea that the worship of this Great Spirit did not originate with the
Peruvian Princes. Mr. Helps[1] also says that a temple
to Pachacamac existed before the time of the Yncas,
and that they artfully connected this Deity with
their own religion, making out that the Sun was his
father, and thus strengthening themselves by alliance
with this primæval Deity. Rivero adopts the same
view, namely that the Gods *Con* and *Pachacamac* were early deities, whose temple was on the
sea-coast, and that the Yncas cunningly adopted
their worship, saying that these gods were sons of
the Sun.[2] There is no adequate authority for these
theories, and they seem to have arisen from a mis-
apprehension of the story as told by early writers.

The inhabitants of the Peruvian coast, called

[1] *Helps*, iii, p. 498. The name of *Con*, given by Mr. Helps,
from Las Casas, as the father of Pachacamac, has originated in
some blunder among the Spanish writers. It is not an Ynca
word at all, and the legend concerning this *Con* has no connection
whatever with any Ynca people. See also *Gomara, Hist. de Las
Indias*, cap. cxxii. The prefix *Con* is found in the names applied
to sacred things by the coast people, and it lingered still longer
in the valleys of Huarochiri. Its meaning is now lost, but it belonged to the coast language. Thus there was a god in Huarochiri called *Coniraya*, and the general name of all small stone
idols in Huarochiri was *Conopa*. See *Avila MS*.

[2] *Antiguedades Peruanas*, p. 144.

Yuncas by their Ynca conquerors, were an entirely
distinct race from the people of the Andes, with a
language differing both in its vocabulary and gram-
matical construction. After long and fierce wars
they were conquered by the Yncas, their language
was superseded by Quichua, many were sent as colonists into the interior, Ynca colonists settled on the
coast, and the nationality of the Yuncas was destroyed. Very little can now be learnt respecting
them. The coast valleys were densely peopled, as is
shown by the fact of ruined towns being always
found on the verge of the desert, so as not to en-
croach on the cultivatable area. They had brought
the art of irrigation to a high state of perfection, and
they adorned the walls of their buildings with richly
coloured paintings. We have no dictionary of their
language, but we have a grammar and vocabulary
by Carrera,[3] and a few specimens of one of its dialects
preserved by Bishop Orè.[4] Of the nature of their
religion we know still less. Avila has recorded
some curious traditions,[5] and it would seem, from
the proceedings of Arriaga, the extirpator of idola-
try, that they were much addicted to sorcery and
fortune-telling.[6] Their gods were made to give

[3] *Arte de la lengua de los valles del Obispado de Truxillo; por
Don Fernando de la Carrera* (Lima, 1644).

[4] The *Mochica* spoken once in the valleys of Huarcu (Cañete),
Runahuanac (Lunahuana), and Chincha. " *Rituale seu Manuale
Peruanum; por Ludovicum Hieronymum Orerium*" (Neapoli, 1607).

[5] In his narrative of the errors, false gods, and other diabolical
rites of the Indians of Huarochiri. MS. in the Biblioteca Nacional
at Madrid, B. 35.

[6] " *Extirpacion de la idolatria de los Indios del Peru; por Pedro*

out oracles, and the shrines became rich and important, in proportion to the credit they attained in forecasting events. Thus, there was a famous oracle in the valley, thence called *Rimac*, or "the Speaker", by the Ynca conquerors ; and a still more renowned one was the fish-god in the city, afterwards called by the Yncas *Pachacamac*, to which pilgrims resorted from all parts of the coast. But this fish-god was not Pachacamac, nor was the word Pachacamac known to the people of the coast before they were conquered by the Yncas. It is an Ynca word, and is wholly foreign to, and unconnected with, the coast language. The priests of the fish-god, it would seem, became famous as fortune-tellers, ; their shrine was resorted to by pilgrims from distant valleys, and a large city grew up around it, on the margin of the sea, and of the rich vale of Lurin. The name of the deity has not been preserved, but it certainly was not Pachacamac.

In course of time the coast valleys were conquered by the Yncas, who gave them Quichua names. Nasca, Pisco, Runahuanac, Pachacamac, Rimac, Huamau, etc., are all pure Quichua names. It seems clear, therefore, that, when the Ynca Garcilasso tells us that the coast lord Cuismancu had adopted the worship of Pachacamac from the Yncas, and had built a temple to him, in which however he placed the fish and fox-gods of the Yuncas, that his ideas were con-

José de Arriaga" (Lima, 1621). The old fanatic says that he punished sixty-three wizards, in the coast valleys.

fused.[7] He assumed that there was a worship of
Pachacamac because the place had received that
name; but the fish and fox-gods are a clear proof that
a Supreme Being was not worshipped there. In short
the word Pachacamac had nothing to do with the religion of the coast people. The worship of the Supreme
Being, under the names of Pachacamac[8] (*Creator of the
World*) and Pachayachachic[9] (*Teacher of the World*),
formed a prominent feature in the religion of the
Yncas. The names occur, and have the first place, in
nearly all the ceremonial prayers of the Yncas given
by Molina.[1] When the Yncas conquered the coast-
city of the fish-god, they assigned to it the name of
Pachacamac, for some reason that has not been preserved, possibly on account of its size and importance.

The Yncas frequently named places after their
deities or sacred festivals. Thus, besides this *Pachacamac*, we have another at Tumebamba, and *Vilca-
ñota*, *Vilca*-pampa, *Vilca*-cunca, *Huaca*-chaca, *Huaca*-
puncu, *Raymi*-pampa, and many more.[2]

[7] *Comm. Real.*, Pt. i, lib. vi, cap. 30. Herrera is still more in
the dark. He says that the Yncas believed in a Creator of all
things called Viracocha, to whom they built a very rich temple
called Pachiamac. Dec. v, lib. iv, cap. 4.

[8] From *Pacha* (the world) and *camac* the participle of *Camani*
(I create). See *G. de la Vega*, i, lib. ii, cap. 22; and lib. v,
cap. 12.

[9] From *Pacha* (the world) and *Yachachic*, participle of *Yacha-
chini* (I teach). See *Acosta*, lib. v, cap. 12; *G. de la Vega*, Pt. i,
lib. v, cap. 18; and *Molina MS.*

[1] *Relacion de las fabulas y ritos de los Yncas, hecha por Christoval de Molina.* MS. at Madrid, B. 35.

[2] *Vilca* is a sacred place, *Huaca* an analogous but more com-
prehensive term, and *Raymi* the great festival of the Sun.

But they never built any temple to Pachacamac, and there never was one to that deity, except at Cuzco. On the summit of the lofty hill, overhanging the town of Pachacamac, they erected a temple of the Sun, which was approached by three wide terraces. Rivero states[3] that the temple of the Sun was not on the top of the hill, but Cieza de Leon[4] distinctly asserts that the loftiest part was set aside as a temple of the Sun. Astete also says that, adjoining the "mosque" (that is, the temple of the fish-god), there was a house of the Sun, situated on a hill, with five surrounding walls. Hernando Pizarro tells us that the store-rooms of gold and the convents of women were at the foot of the hill, and that the chief priest and the building containing the fish-god (devil, as he calls it) were on the terrace platform above. Higher up there were two other wide terraces, and the temple of the Sun was on the summit.

The Yncas built a temple of the Sun on the hill top ; though, in accordance with their usual policy, they allowed the wooden fish idol to remain in its shrine below ; which they even condescended to consult as an oracle, from conciliatory motives. But its importance waned after the Ynca conquest, the pilgrims fell off in numbers, and the town began to lose its citizens. When Hernando Pizarro arrived in 1533, the greater part of the outer wall had fallen, and there were many houses in ruins. Here is an additional proof that this was not a temple to

---

[3] *Antiq. Per.*, p. 291.
[4] See my translation, p. 253.

the Ynca deity Pachacamac, "the only temple in
Peru dedicated to the Supreme Being". If such
had been the case, its importance would have increased, and not diminished, after the conquest by
the Yncas, in whose prayers the Creator ever had
the first place. There is no reason for supposing
that pilgrims ever resorted to the shrine of the fish-
god from any part of the empire of the Yncas, except
the coast valleys; and the diversity of skulls alleged
to have been found among the ruins is sufficiently
accounted for by the presence of *mitimaes* or colonists,
and by the marches of Ynca armies.[5]

The conclusions I have formed are, that the worship of Pachacamac, the Creator of the World, was
a part of the Ynca religious belief; and that it was
wholly unconnected with the coast Indians; that
there never was any temple to Pachacamac at the
place on the coast to which the Yncas gave that
name, for some reason now forgotten; that the
natives worshipped a fish-god there under a name
now lost, which became famous as an oracle, and
attracted pilgrims; and that, when the Yncas conquered the place, they raised a temple to the Sun,
on the summit of the hill commanding the city of
the fish-god, whence the glorious luminary could be
seen to descend behind the distant horizon, and
bathe the ocean in floods of light. These conclusions
are supported by the writings of Garcilasso de la
Vega and Cieza de Leon, and by the report of
Astete; and they agree with all that is recorded of

[5] See my translation of *Cieza de Leon*. Note, p. 252.

the religious belief of the Yncas, and with the few
facts that can be gathered, from various sources,
touching the Yuncas or coast Indians.

The present Editor examined the ruins of Pachacamac, in much detail, in 1853 and again in 1854,
and made a plan of them. He again visited them
on the 19th of February, 1860, accompanied by an
Irish chieftain and two Englishmen. We ascended
the terraces on horseback to the platform of the
temple of the Sun ; where the old Catholic chieftain
broke out in praise of the Yncas. We reminded him
of their heresy, but he repeated, as he drained his
sherry flask, " Here is to the Yncas ! God rest their
souls in peace !" We rode back through the narrow
streets to Lurin, and, in memory of the event, one
of our party wrote the following lines, contrasting
the Catholic Hernando Pizarro of the sixteenth, with
the Catholic Hibernian of the nineteenth century.

> The sunlight glanced from helm and spear
>   Upon the terraced height,
> And awe-struck crowds had gathered round
>   Beneath the temple bright.
>
> High on the ruined altar stone
>   The iron conqueror stood,
> And o'er the broken idol held
>   Outstretch'd the holy rood.
>
> And as he preach'd God's truth, his brow
>   Darker and darker grew,
> And the people feared the bloodstain'd man,
>   And they feared his bloodstain'd crew.
>
> For his speech was cruel and fierce to them,
>   And hard to understand,

As he cursed the children of the Sun,
   The rulers of the land.

       *   *   *   *

Full many a year is passed and gone
   Since that strange scene befell,
Of many a tale of blood and woe
   The silent ruins tell.

We stood upon the temple wall,
   And fierce the sunlight beat
Upon the sand that compassed round
   The city at our feet.

The ruin'd terrace gardens told
   Of splendour passed away,
And bleaching in the Sun, the bones
   Of Priest and Warrior lay.

Then one who held the ancient creed
   Of him who preached of yore,
And bowed before the self-same sign,
   The cross the conqueror bore.

Raised high the wine cup in his hand,
   " We'll drink the noble dead !
The Princely Rulers of the land !
   God rest their souls," he said.

As through the silent streets below
   We rode among the dead,
We mused which held the faith of Him
   Whose blood for all was shed.

Or he who cursed the Pagan Kings,
   And bade their empire cease,
Or he who prayed above their graves,
   "God rest their souls in peace".

A TRUE ACCOUNT

OF THE PROVINCE

OF CUZCO,

Called New Castille, conquered by *Francisco Pizarro*,
captain to His Majesty the Emperor,
our Master.

Dedicated to His Majesty the Emperor by

FRANCISCO XERES,

Native of the most noble and most loyal town of Seville, Secretary
to the said Captain in all the Provinces and Countries
conquered in New Castille, and one of the first
conquerors of that country.

SALAMANCA:

1547.

Second Edition.

NARRATIVE OF THE CONQUEST OF PERU.

BY

FRANCISCO XERES.

BECAUSE the Divine Providence; and the fortune of Cæsar; and the prudence, fortitude, military discipline, labours, perilous navigations, and battles of the Spaniards, vassals of the most invincible Emperor of the Roman Empire, our natural King and Lord, will cause joy to the faithful and terror to the infidels; for the glory of God our Lord and for the service of the Catholic Imperial Majesty; it has seemed good to me to write this narrative, and to send it to your Majesty, that all may have a knowledge of what is here related. It will be to the glory of God, because they have conquered and brought to our holy Catholic Faith so vast a number of heathens, aided by His holy guidance. It will be to the honour of our Emperor because, by reason of his great power and good fortune, such events happened in his time. It will give joy to the faithful that such battles have been won, such provinces discovered and conquered, such riches brought home for the King and for themselves; and that such terror has been spread among the infidels, such admiration excited in all mankind.

For when, either in ancient or modern times, have such great exploits been achieved by so few against so many; over so many climes, across so many seas, over such distances by land, to subdue the unseen and unknown? Whose deeds can be compared with those of Spain? Not surely those of the Jews, nor of the Greeks, nor even of the

B

Romans, of whom more is written than of any other people.
For though the Romans subjugated so many provinces, yet
they did so with an equal number of troops or but slightly
less in number, and the lands were known, and well supplied
with provisions, and their captains and armies were paid.
But our Spaniards, being few in number, never having more
than two hundred or three hundred men together, and sometimes only a hundred and even fewer (only once, and that
twenty years ago, with the Captain Pedrarias, was there the
larger number of fifteen hundred men); and those who have
come at different times being neither paid nor pressed, but
serving of their own free wills and at their own costs, have,
in our times, conquered more territory than has ever been
known before, or than all the faithful and infidel princes possessed. Moreover, they supported themselves on the savage
food of the people, who had no knowledge of bread or wine,
suffering on a diet of herbs, fruits, and roots. Yet they
have made conquests which are now known to all the world.
I will only write, at present, of what befell in the conquest
of New Castille; and I will not write much, in order to
avoid prolixity.

The South Sea having been discovered, and the inhabitants of Tierra Firme having been conquered and pacified,
the Governor Pedrarias de Avila founded and settled the
cities of Panama and of Nata, and the town of Nombre de
Dios. At this time the Captain Francisco Pizarro, son of
the Captain Gonzalo Pizarro, a knight of the city of Truxillo,
was living in the city of Panama; possessing his house, his
farm, and his Indians, as one of the principal people of the
land, which indeed he always was, having distinguished
himself in the conquest and settling, and in the service of
his Majesty. Being at rest and in repose, but full of zeal
to continue his labours and to perform other more distinguished services for the royal crown, he sought permission
from Pedrarias to discover that coast of the South Sea to

the eastward. He spent a large part of his fortune on a good ship which he built, and on necessary supplies for the voyage, and he set out from the city of Panama on the 14th day of the month of November, in the year 1524.[1] He had a hundred and twelve Spaniards in his company, besides some Indian servants. He commenced a voyage in which they suffered many hardships, the season being winter and unpropitious. I shall omit many things that happened which might be tedious, and will only relate the notable events, and those that are most to the purpose.

Seventy days after leaving Panama they landed at a port which was afterwards named Port Famine. They had previously landed at many ports, but had abandoned them because there were no inhabitants. The captain and eighty men remained in this port (the remainder having died); and because their provisions had come to an end, and there were none in that land, he sent the ship, with the sailors and an officer,[2] to the Isle of Pearls (which is in the jurisdiction of Panama) to obtain supplies, thinking that, at the end of ten or twelve days, they would return with succour. But Fortune is always, or generally, adverse; and the ship never returned for forty-seven days, during which time the captain and his companions subsisted on a sea-weed that they found on the shore, collecting it with much trouble. Some of them, being sorely weakened, died. They also fed on some very bitter palm fruits. During the absence of the ship, in going and returning, more than twenty men died. When the ship returned with supplies, the captain and mariners related how, when the supplies did not come, they had eaten a tanned cow-hide which had been used to cover the pump. They boiled it and divided it amongst themselves. The survivors were refreshed with the supplies brought by the ship, consisting of maize and pigs; and

[1] Herrera gives the same date. Cieza de Leon and Garcilasso de la Vega have 1525.   [2] Named Montenegro.

the captain set out to continue his voyage. He came to a town on the sea-shore, built in a strong position and surrounded by pallisades. Here he found provisions in abundance, but the inhabitants fled from the town. The next day a number of armed men came. They were warlike and well armed ; while the Christians were reduced by hunger and their previous hardships. The Christians were defeated and their captain received seven wounds, the slightest of which was dangerous. The Indians, who had wounded him, left him because they thought he was dead. Seventeen other men were wounded with him, and five were killed. Seeing the result of this disaster, and the small chance of being able to cure and revive his people, the captain embarked and returned to the land of Panama, landing at an Indian village near the island of Pearls, called Chuchama.[2] Thence he sent the ship to Panama,[3] for she had become unseaworthy by reason of the *teredo ;* and all that had befallen was reported to Pedrarias, while the captain remained behind to refresh himself and his companions.

When the ship arrived at Panama it was found that, a few days before, the Captain Diego de Almagro had sailed in search of the Captain Pizarro, his companion, with another ship and seventy men. He sailed as far as the village where the Captain Pizarro was defeated, and the Captain Almagro had another encounter with the Indians of that place, and was also defeated. He lost an eye, and many Christians were wounded ; but, nevertheless, the Indians abandoned the village, which was set on fire. They again set out, and followed the coast until they came to a great river, which they called San Juan[4] because they arrived there on his day. They there found signs of gold, but there being

---

[2] The province of Chuchama was discovered by Pascual de Andagoya in 1522. See my translation of Andagoya, p. 40.

[3] In command of his treasurer, Nicolas de Ribera.

[4] A few miles north of the port of Buenaventura, in New Granada.

no traces of the Captain Pizarro, the Captain Almagro returned to Chuchama, where he found his comrade. They agreed that the Captain Almagro should go to Panama, repair the ships, collect more men to continue the enterprise, and defray the expenses, which amounted to more than ten thousand *castellanos*.[5] At Panama much obstruction was caused by Pedrarias and others, who said that the voyage should not be persisted in, and that his Majesty would not be served by it. The Captain Almagro, with the authority given him by his comrade, was very constant in prosecuting the work he had commenced, and he required the Governor Pedrarias not to obstruct him, because he believed, with the help of God, that his Majesty would be well served by that voyage. Thus Pedrarias was forced to allow him to engage men. He set out from Panama with a hundred and ten men; and went to the place where Pizarro waited with another fifty of the first hundred and ten who sailed with him, and of the seventy who accompanied Almagro when he went in search. The other hundred and thirty were dead. The two captains, in their two ships, sailed with a hundred and sixty men, and coasted along the land.[6] When they thought they saw signs of habitations, they went on shore in three canoes they had with them, rowed by sixty men, and so they sought for provisions.

They continued to sail in this way for three years, suffering great hardships from hunger and cold. The greater part of the crews died of hunger, insomuch that there were not fifty surviving, and during all those three years they discovered no good land. All was swamp and inundated country, without inhabitants. The good country they discovered was as far as the river San Juan, where the Captain

---

[5] The value of the *castellano* varied. At this time it was worth about eight shillings.

[6] Their experienced and resolute Pilot was Bartolomé Ruiz, a native of Moguer, in Andalusia.

Pizarro remained with the few survivors, sending a captain[7] with the smaller ship to discover some good land further along the coast. He sent the other ship, with the Captain Diego de Almagro, to Panama to get more men, because with the two vessels together and so few men no discovery could be made, and the people died. The ship that was sent to discover, returned at the end of seventy days to the river of San Juan, where the Captain Pizarro remained with his people, and reported to him what had befallen. They had arrived at the village of Cancebi, which is on this coast, and before they reached it, the crew of the ship had seen other inhabited places, very rich in gold and silver, and inhabited by more intelligent people than they had previously met with. They brought six persons that they might learn the language of the Spaniards, together with gold, silver, and cloths.[8] The Captain and his comrades received this news with so much joy, that they forgot all their former sufferings, and the expenses they had incurred, and conceived a strong desire to see that land which appeared to be so inviting. As soon as the Captain Almagro arrived from Panama with a ship laden with men and horses, the two ships, with their commanders and all their people, set out from the river San Juan, to go to that newly-discovered land. But the navigation was difficult, they were detained so long[9] that the provisions were exhausted, and the people were obliged to go on shore in search of supplies. The

---

[7] Ruiz, the Pilot.

[8] Ruiz discovered the bay of San Mateo and the isle of Gallo, and encountered a native raft, laden with merchandise : vases and mirrors of silver, and cotton and woollen cloths. Some of the people on board were natives of Tumbez ; and he took six into his vessel, intending to make them learn Spanish, and become interpreters. The furthest point reached by Ruiz was the Cape of Passaos, and he was thus the first European to cross the line in the Pacific Ocean.

[9] They had constant northerly winds, with heavy squalls, and storms of thunder and lightning.

ships reached the bay of San Mateo, and some villages to which the Spaniards gave the name of Santiago. Next they came to the villages of Tacamez,[1] on the sea coast further on. These villages were seen by the Christians to be large and well peopled; and when ninety Spaniards had advanced a league beyond the villages of Tacamez,[2] more than ten thousand Indian warriors encountered them; but seeing that the Christians intended no evil, and did not wish to take their goods, but rather to treat them peacefully with much love, the Indians desisted from war. In this land there were abundant supplies, and the people led well-ordered lives, the villages having their streets and squares. One village had more than three thousand houses, and others were smaller.

It seemed to the Captains and to the other Spaniards that nothing could be done in that land by reason of the smallness of their number, which rendered them unable to cope with the Indians. So they agreed to load the ships with the supplies to be found in the villages, and to return to an island called Gallo,[3] where they would be safe until the ships arrived at Panama with the news of what had been discovered, and to apply to the Governor for more men, in order that the Captains might be able to continue their undertaking, and conquer the land. Captain Almagro went in the ships. Many persons had written to the Governor entreating him to order the crews to return to Panama, saying that it was impossible to endure more hardships than they had suffered during the last three years.[4] The Governor ordered that all those who wished to go to Panama

[1] Atacames, on the coast of modern Ecuador.

[2] The modern Atacames.

[3] In the bay of Tumaco, just on the modern frontier dividing New Granada from Ecuador. It had already been discovered by the Pilot Ruiz.

[4] See *Herrera*, Dec. III, lib. x, cap. 3; *Garcilasso de la Vega*, Pt. II; and *Cieza de Leon*, cap. cxix.

might do so, while those who desired to continue the discoveries were at liberty to remain. Sixteen men stayed
with Pizarro,[5] and all the rest went back in the ships to

[5] Thus simply does Pizarro's Secretary tell the story of this famous
resolution. A ship was sent from Panama, by the Governor, under the
command of an officer named Tafur, to take back those who wished to
return ; while those who chose to remain with Pizarro were allowed to
do so. Garcilasso says that, when Pizarro saw his men electing to return in the ship, he drew his sword and made a long line on the ground
with the point. Then, turning to his men, he said: "Gentlemen! This
line signifies labour, hunger, thirst, fatigue, wounds, sickness, and every
other kind of danger that must be encountered in this conquest, until
life is ended. Let those who have the courage to meet and overcome the
dangers of this heroic achievement cross the line in token of their resolution and as a testimony that they will be my faithful companions.
And let those who feel unworthy of such daring return to Panama ; for
I do not wish to put force upon any man. I trust in God that, for his
greater honour and glory, his eternal Majesty will help those who remain with me, though they be few, and that we shall not feel the want
of those who forsake us." On hearing this speech the Spaniards began
to go on board with all speed, lest anything should happen to detain
them.

Herrera tells the story differently. He says that Tafur stationed himself in one part of the vessel and, drawing a line, placed Pizarro and the
soldiers on the other side of it. He then told those who wished to return
to Panama to come over to him, and those who would remain to stay on
Pizarro's side of the line.

Of these two accounts, that of Garcilasso is far more likely to be true;
for it is very improbable that they would all have embarked before the
election was made. It would naturally be made on the beach before
they went on board.

The authorities also differ as to the number of men who crossed the
line and remained with Pizarro. Cieza de Leon, Gomara, Herrera, and
Garcilasso say there were thirteen; Zarate gives the number at twelve;
Xeres at sixteen. In the Capitulation for the Conquest of Peru, made
by Francisco Pizarro with Queen Juana on July 26th, 1529, there is
the following paragraph : "Remembering the great services that were
performed in the said discovery by Bartolomé Ruiz, Cristoval de Peralta,
Pedro de Candia, Domingo de Soria Luce, Nicolas de Ribera, Francisco
de Cuellar, Alonzo de Molina, Pedro Alcon, Garcia de Jerez, Anton de
Carrion, Alonzo Briceño, Martin de Paz, and Juan de la Torre ; and
because you have besought and prayed for the favour, it is our will and
pleasure to grant it, as by these presents we do grant to such of them as

Panama. The Captain Pizarro was on that island for five months, when one of the ships returned, in which he continued the discoveries for a hundred leagues further down the coast. They found many villages, and great riches;

are not Hidalgos, that they shall be Hidalgos acknowledged in those parts, and that in all our Indies they shall enjoy rank and immunities and such other privileges as belong to acknowledged Hidalgos, and to those who now are Hidalgos we grant knighthood of gilt spurs."

It has always been supposed that these were the men who crossed the line, and hence their number has been placed at thirteen. But it is not asserted in the Capitulation that the men whose names are given in it were those who crossed the line, and it might be that Pizarro, in asking favours for his most faithful companions, on the one hand omitted one or more of those who crossed the line, and on the other included some who did not take part in that transaction, but who joined him afterwards. Herrera gives the names of the thirteen in the Capitulation, and says that one was a Mulatto. Zarate gives nine names, all of which are in the above paragraph of the Capitulation except one, Alonzo de Truxillo. Zarate's nine are—Pedro de Candia, Bartolomé Ruiz, Nicolas de Ribera, Juan de la Torre, Alonzo Briceño, Cristoval de Peralta, Alonzo de Truxillo, Francisco de Cuellar, and Alonzo de Molina. Balboa adds two more, Juan Roldan and Blas de Atienza. Garcilasso gives yet two more, whom he knew personally. He says that the correct name of Zarate's Alonzo de Truxillo was Diego de Truxillo; that there were two Riberas, one the Nicolas of the Capitulation, and the other Geronimo or Alonzo, he is not certain which, whom he knew personally; and that Francisco Rodriguez de Villafuerte, a citizen of Cuzco, whom he also knew personally, was the first to walk across the line.

In these conflicting lists, the names of Ruiz, Candia, Peralta, Briceño, Ribera, Torre, Cuellar, and Molina, are those on which all are agreed. The Capitulation makes up the thirteen with Soria Luce, Alcon, Jerez, Carrion, and Paz; which five names Zarate and Garcilasso omit. Zarate adds Truxillo. Garcilasso gives him also, and adds another Ribera and Villa-Fuerte. Balboa adds Roldan and Atienza.

Xeres had access to the best information, and I believe his number of sixteen to be correct; including the Pilot Ruiz, who returned to Panama to obtain another vessel. The three additional names of Zarate and Garcilasso may be supposed to have been omitted in the Capitulation, either intentionally by Pizarro for some reason of his own, or accidentally. The correct list of sixteen will then stand as follows: [c. before a name meaning that it occurs in the Capitulation and Herrera; z. that it is given by Zarate; and G. by Garcilasso.] The two additional names of

and they brought away more specimens of gold, silver, and cloths than had been found before, which were presented by the natives. The Captain returned because the time granted

Balboa are no doubt inserted by mistake; but not so those of Garcilasso; for he knew the men personally.

(c. z. b. g.) 1. *Bartolomé Ruiz*, of Moguer, the Pilot.

(c. z. b. g.) 2. *Pedro de Candia*, a Greek. He commanded Pizarro's artillery, consisting of two falconets; and was an able and experienced officer. After Pizarro's death he joined the younger Almagro, who killed him on suspicion of treachery at the battle of Chupas. He left a half-caste son, who was at school with Garcilasso at Cuzco.

(c. z. g.) 3. *Cristoval de Peralta*, a native of Baeza. He was one of the first twelve citizens of Lima, when that city was founded by Pizarro in 1535.

(c. z. b. g.) 4. *Alonzo Briceño*, a native of Benavente. He was at the division of Atahualpa's ransom, and received the share of a cavalry captain.

(c. z. b. g.) 5. *Nicolas de Ribera*, the Treasurer, was one of the first twelve citizens of Lima, when Pizarro founded that city on January 18th, 1535. He passed through all the stormy period of the civil wars in Peru. He deserted from Gonzalo Pizarro to Gasca, and was afterwards Captain of the Guard of the Royal Seal. He eventually settled near Cuzco, and left children to inherit his estates.

(c. z. b. g.) 6. *Juan de la Torre* was a staunch adherent of Gonzalo Pizarro in after years, to whom he deserted when serving under the ill-fated Viceroy Blasco Nuñez de Vela. He carried his ferocious enmity to the Viceroy so far as to insult his dead body, and, pulling the hairs out of his beard, stuck them in his hatband. He married the daughter of an Indian chief near Puerto Viejo, and acquired great wealth. He was captain of arquebusiers for Gonzalo Pizarro until 1548, and after the battle of Sacsahuana he was hanged by order of La Gasca.

(c. z. g.) 7. *Francisco de Cuellar*, a native of Cuellar. Nothing more is known of him.

(c. z. g.) 8. *Alonzo de Molina*, a native of Ubeda. He afterwards landed at Tumbez, where it was arranged that he should remain until Pizarro's return; but he died in the interval.

(c.) 9. *Domingo de Soria Luce*. Nothing more is known of him.

(c.) 10. *Pedro Alcon*. He afterwards landed on the coast of Peru, fell in love with a Peruvian lady, and refused to come on board again. So the Pilot Ruiz was obliged to knock him down with

by the Governor had expired, and the last day of the period
had been reached, when he entered the port of Panama.[6]

The two Captains were so ruined that they could no longer
prosecute their undertaking, owing a large sum of *pesos de
oro*. The Captain Francisco Pizarro was only able to bor-
row a little more than a thousand *castellanos*[7] among his
friends, with which sum he went to Castille, and gave an

an oar, and he was put in irons on the lower deck. Nothing
more is known of him.

(c.) 11. *Garcia de Jerez* (or *Jaren*). He appears to have made a
statement on the subject of the heroism of Pizarro and his companions at Panama on August 3rd, 1529. (*Doc. Ined.*, tom. xxvi,
p. 260; quoted by *Helps*, iii, p. 446.)

(c.) 12. *Anton de Carrion.* Nothing further is known of him.

(c.) 13. *Martin de Paz.* Nothing further is known of him.

(z. G.) 14. *Diego de Truxillo* (*Alonzo*, according to Zarate). He
was afterwards personally known to Garcilasso at Cuzco. Diego
de Truxillo appears to have written an account of the discovery
of Peru, which is still in manuscript. "*Didacus de Truxillo.
Relacion de la tierra que descubrió con Dom Francisco Pizarro
en el Peru.*" (*Antonio*, ii, 645.) Antonio quotes from the "*Bib-
liotheca Indica*" of Leon Pinelo.

(G.) 15. *Geromino* or *Alonzo Ribera.* He was settled at Lima, where
he had children.

(G.) 16. *Francisco Rodriquez de Villa-Fuerte*, the first to cross the
line. Afterwards a citizen of Cuzco, having been present at the
siege by Ynca Manco, and at the battle of Las Salinas. Garcilasso knew him, and once rode with him from Cuzco to Quispi-
cancha, when he recounted many reminiscences of his stirring
life. He was still living at Cuzco in 1560, a rich and influential
citizen.

[6] The Governor of Panama allowed one vessel to go, under the com-
mand of the Pilot Ruiz, with positive orders to return in six months.
Pizarro sailed in her from the isle of Gorgona, and came to the gulf of
Guayaquil, after a voyage of twenty days. He landed on the island of
Santa Clara or Muerto, and then stood across to the town of Tumbez.
He then explored the Peruvian coast as far as the river of Santa. See
the note in my translation of *Cieza de Leon*, p. 420. Pizarro took two
Peruvians from Tumbez, who became interpreters, but very bad ones,
as they spoke execrable Spanish and worse Quichua. One was named
Filipillo by the Spaniards, the other Martinillo.

[7] £400.

account to his Majesty of the great and signal services he
had performed ; in reward for which he was granted the
government and command of that land,[8] and the habit of
Santiago ; certain magisterial powers, and aids towards the
coast were given by his Majesty as Emperor and King, who
ever shows favour to those who work in his royal service,
as he always has done. For this cause others have been
animated with zeal to spend their estates in his royal service, discovering in that South Sea, and over all the ocean,
lands and provinces so distant from these kingdoms of
Castille.

When the Adelantado Francisco Pizarro was nominated
by his Majesty, he sailed from the port of San Lucar[9] with
a fleet,[1] and with a fair wind and without accident, arrived
at the port of Nombre de Dios. Thence he went, with his
forces, to the city of Panama, where he encountered many
difficulties and obstructions intended to prevent him from
going to people the land he had discovered, according to his
Majesty's orders. But he resolutely continued his preparations, and sailed from Panama with as many people as he
could collect, being a hundred and eighty men, with thirty-
seven horses, in three ships.[2] His voyage was so success-
ful that in thirteen days he arrived at the bay of San Mateo,
though, when they began this enterprise, they could never

[8] The Capitulation made by Francisco Pizarro with Queen Juana, is
dated at Toledo, on July 26th, 1529. The text is given by Quintana in
his *Vidas*, p. 176, and by Prescott in an Appendix, ii, p. 447. The chief
right of discovery and conquest of the country for two hundred leagues
south of the island of Santiago or Puna, which was called New Castille,
was secured to Pizarro, with the title of Governor for life. Almagro
was made Commander of Tumbez, Ruiz received the title of Grand
Pilot of the Southern Ocean, and Candia was made Captain of Artillery.
Pizarro received the habit of Santiago.   [9] In January 1530.

[1] He took out with him four brothers: Hernando, the eldest, and only
legitimate son of his father ; Gonzalo and Juan, like Francisco himself,
illegitimate sons; and Francisco Martin de Alcantara, a son of his mother
but not of his father.   [2] In January 1531.

reach it during more than two years. There he landed the
people and horses, and they marched along the shore, finding all the inhabitants in arms against them. They continued their march until they reached a large village called
Coaque, which they entered, for the inhabitants had not
risen, as in the other villages. There they took fifteen thousand *pesos*[3] *de oro*, fifteen hundred *marcs*[4] of silver, and many
emeralds which were not then known as, nor held to be,
precious stones. Hence the Spaniards obtained them from
the Indians for cloths and other things. In this village
they took the Cacique or Lord of the place, with some
of his people, and they found much cloth of different kinds,
and abundant supplies, sufficient to maintain the Spaniards
for three or four years.

The Governor despatched the three ships from Coaque
to the city of Panama and to Nicaragua, to get more men
and horses, in order to secure the conquest and settling of
the land. The Governor remained there with his people,
resting for some days until two of the ships returned from
Panama with twenty-six horsemen and thirty foot soldiers.
On their arrival the Governor set out, with the horse and
foot, marching along the sea coast, which was well peopled,
and placing all the villages under the dominion of his
Majesty; for their lords, with one accord, came out into the
roads to receive the Governor, without making any opposition. The Governor, far from doing them any harm or
showing any anger, received them all lovingly, and they
were taught some things touching our holy Catholic Faith,
by the monks who accompanied the expedition. Thus the
Governor advanced with the Spaniards, until they reached
an island called Puna, to which the Spaniards gave the
name of Santiago.[5] It is two leagues from the main land;

---

[3] A *peso* of gold was worth a *castellano* or about eight shillings.
[4] A *marc* was eight ounces.
[5] In the gulf of Guayaquil. Ternaux Compans, in a note, makes the

and, being populous, and rich, and yielding abundant supplies, the Governor crossed over to it in two ships, and in
balsas[6] of wood which the Indians make, on which the
horses were carried over.

The Governor was received on this island by the Lord
with much joy, and many presents of provisions, which were
brought out on the road, together with musical instruments
that the natives use for their recreation.   This island is
fifteen leagues round.   It is fertile and populous, and contains many villages, ruled by seven chiefs, one of whom is
lord over the others.   This chief gave a quantity of gold
and silver to the Governor of his own free will, and, as it
was winter, the Governor and his people rested on that
island ; for he could not have advanced in the rains without
serious detriment.   Several of those who were sick recovered
before the rainy season was over.   The natural inclination
of the Indians is not to obey or serve any foreigner, unless
they are obliged to do so by force.   This Cacique had peacefully lived with the Governor, and had become a vassal of
his Majesty; yet it became known, through the interpreters
of the Governor, that he had assembled all his warriors, and
that for many days they had been employed in making arms.
This was also observed with their own eyes by the Spaniards,
in the village where they and the Cacique were lodged.
Many armed Indians were found in the house of the Cacique

extraordinary mistake of turning the native name of Puna into *Pugna*,
which he translates into " Fight", and identifying it with the island of
Gorgona.   Puna is three hundred and seventy miles south of Gorgona,
and far more by the course a vessel must take round the coast.   See an
account of the conquest of the island of Puna by the Yncas, in my
translation of Garcilasso de la Vega, ii, p. 429.

    [6] Zarate thus describes these balsas (lib. i, cap. vi, p. 6): " They are
made of long light poles fastened across two other poles.   Those on the
top are always an odd number, generally five, and sometimes seven or
nine : the centre poles being longer than the others, where the rower
sits.   Thus the shape of the *balsa* is like that of a hand stretched out,

and in the other houses, waiting until all the islanders were
assembled before they attacked the Christians in the following night. When the Governor had received this information from his secret spies, he ordered the Cacique, his three
sons, and other principal men to be taken prisoners, and
the Spaniards attacked the armed Indians and killed several, while the others fled, abandoning the village. The
house of the Cacique and some others were pillaged, some
gold and silver and much cloth being found in them. During
that night very careful watch was kept in the camp of the
Christians, their number being sixty horse and a hundred
foot. Before next day dawned they heard warlike cries,
and soon a great number of Indians was seen to approach,
all the men being armed and playing warlike instruments.
They advanced in several bodies, and attacked the Christian
camp. By this time it was daylight, and the Governor
ordered his men to assault the enemy with vigour. Some
Christians and horses were wounded; but, as our Lord
favours and succours those who are engaged in his service,
the Indians were defeated, and turned their backs. The
horse-soldiers followed them, wounding and killing several.
The Christians returned to the camp, because the horses
were tired, the pursuit having continued from morning
until noon.

On a following day the Governor sent his troops in detachments over the island to search for their enemies, and make
war upon them, which they continued to do during twenty
days; so that the Indians were well punished. Three principal men, who were prisoners with the chief, were accused
by him of having advised and arranged the treason, while
he himself did not wish to join it but was unable to control

with the length of the fingers diminishing from the centre. On the
top some boards are fixed, to prevent the men from getting wet. There
are *balsas* which will hold fifty men. They are navigated with a sail
and oars."

these leaders.   The Governor executed judgment upon
them, burning some, and beheading the others.

By reason of the insurrection and treason of the Cacique
and Indians of the island of Santiago, war was made upon
them until they abandoned their island and crossed over to
the main land.   But, seeing that the island was rich and
fertile, the Governor set the Cacique at liberty that he might
gather his scattered people together and re-settle the island,
so that it might not be ruined.   The Cacique was content
to serve his Majesty henceforward, by reason of the kind
treatment he received in prison.   The Governor then departed with as many Spaniards and horses as his three ships
would hold, for the town of Tumbez,[7] leaving behind some
troops with a captain, for whom the ships were to return.[8]
But, in order that the passage might be effected more
quickly, the Governor caused the Cacique to provide *balsas*,
in which three Christians went with a supply of cloths to
Tumbez.   In three days the ships reached the coast at
Tumbez, and when the Governor landed, he found that the
inhabitants were in arms.   He learnt from some captive
Indians that the people had risen and seized the Christians
and cloths that came in the *balsas*.[9]   As soon as the people
and horses were landed, the Governor ordered the ships to
return for those who were left on the island.   He and his
troops lodged in the village of the Cacique, in two strong
houses built like a fortress.   The Governor then ordered
the Spaniards to explore the country, and to ascend a river

[7] Two vessels, with a reinforcement commanded by Hernando de
Soto, arrived while Pizarro was on the island of Puna.

[8] This was Sebastian de Belalcazar, the future conqueror of Quito,
and Governor of Popayan.

[9] There were four *balsas*.   In one were Francisco Martin de Alcantara, Juan Pizarro, and Alonzo de Mena; in another, Hernando de Soto;
in the third, Alonzo de Toro; and in the fourth, Hurtado, a brother of
Alonzo de Toro, and a soldier.   The three in the latter were seized by
the Indians and murdered.—*Herrera*.

which flows between those villages, that they might get
tidings of the three Christians who were sent in the *balsas;*
in the hope of finding them before they were killed by the
Indians. But, although the Spaniards used much diligence
in exploring the land from the first hour that they came on
shore, they could neither hear nor see anything of the three
Christians. The Spaniards put all the provisions they could
collect in two *balsas,* and they captured some Indians, from
among whom the Governor sent messengers to the Cacique,[1]
and to some principal chiefs, requiring them, on the part
of his Majesty, to make peace and deliver up the three
Christians alive, without having injured them ; in which case
they would be received as vassals of his Majesty, although
they had been transgressors. If they refused, he threatened
to make war upon them with fire and sword, until they were
destroyed.

Some days elapsed, and the Indians not only kept away,
but showed signs of pride and made forts on the other side
of the river, which had increased in size and could not be
forded. They invited the Spaniards to come across, and
told them that they had already killed their three companions.

As soon as all the men had arrived, who were left on the
island, the Governor ordered a great raft of wood to be
made, for the easier passage of the river. He sent forty
horse and eighty foot across with a captain, and they continued to be ferried over on the raft from morning until evening. The captain had orders to make war upon the Indians,
because they were rebels and had slain the Christians ; and,
after they had suffered such punishment as their offence
deserved, they were to be received peacefully in accordance
with the commands of his Majesty. So the captain set out
with his troops, and after he had crossed the river, he took

---

[1] The name of the Chief of Tumbez was Chillemasa, according to
Herrera. But see next page.

guides with him, and marched right towards the place where
the Indians were encamped. At dawn he attacked the
camp where they lodged, and continued the pursuit all that
day, killing and wounding them, and making prisoners of all
he could overtake. Towards night the Christians assembled
at a village. Next morning the Spaniards marched in detachments in search of their enemies, and they again received punishment. When the captain saw that the harm
they had received was sufficient, he sent messengers to pro-
pose terms of peace to the chief. The chief of the province,
which is called Quillimasa, sent one of his principal men
back with the messengers, who made this reply—that "by
reason of the great fear he had of the Spaniards the chief
had not come himself, but that if he was assured that he
would not be killed, he would come peacefully." The captain answered the messenger that "he would not be received
badly, nor would he be injured, that he might come without
fear as the Governor would receive him as a vassal of his
Majesty, and would pardon the fault he had committed."
With this assurance, though in great terror, the chief, with
some principal men, came, and the captain received them
joyfully, saying that "no harm would be done to those who
came peacefully, though they had been in rebellion ; that as
he had come, no more war would be made ; and that the
people might return to their villages." Afterwards he ordered the supplies he had found to be taken across the
river, and he, with his Spaniards, returned to the place
where he had left the Governor, taking the chief and the
principal Indians with him. He reported what had taken
place to the Governor, who gave thanks to our Lord for
having granted a victory, without any Christian being
wounded. He then told them to seek rest. The Governor
asked the chief :—"Why he, who had been so well treated,
had risen and killed the Christians ; when many of his
people had been restored to him, whom the Cacique of the

Island had captured ;[2] and when the captains who had burnt
his villages had been given up to him to receive punishment,
in the belief that he was faithful, and would be grateful for
these benefits ?" The Cacique answered—"I knew that
certain of my principal men brought the three Christians in
the *balsas*, and killed them, but I had no concern in it,
though I feared that the blame would be put upon me."
The Governor replied—"Let those principal men be brought
to me, and send the people back to their villages." The
Cacique then sent for the people and for the principal men,
and said that he could not see those who had killed the
Christians, because they had left the country. After the
Governor had been there for some days, he saw that the
Indian murderers could not be secured, and that the town
of Tumbez was destroyed. It seemed to have been an important place, judging from some edifices it contained.
Among them were two houses, one of which was surrounded
by two circuits of earthen wall. It had open courts and
rooms, and doors for defence, and was a good fortress
against Indians. The natives say that these edifices were
abandoned by reason of a great pestilence, and by reason of
the war that was waged by the Cacique of the island.[3] As
there were no Indians in this district except those who were
subject to the above-mentioned chief, the Governor resolved
to continue his march with some cavalry and foot soldiers,
in search of another more populous province, with a view to
sending people to settle in the town of Tumbez. So he set
out, leaving a Lieutenant with the Christians who remained
in charge of the stores ;[4] and the Cacique remained at peace,
assembling the people in the villages.

[2] Pizarro found two natives of Tumbez in the island of Puna. He
had set them at liberty, in the expectation that they would be useful to
him in their own land.—*Gomara, Hist. de las Indias*, cap. cxii.

[3] For an account of Tumbez and its inhabitants, see my translation
of *Cieza de Leon*, p. 212.

[4] The Contador Antonio Navarro and the Treasurer Alonzo Riquelme
remained behind at Tumbez.

c 2

On the first day that the Governor departed from Tumbez, which was the 16th day of May, 1532, he arrived at a small village, and on the third day he reached a village among hills, and the Cacique, who was Lord of that village, was called Juan. Here they rested for three days, and in three more days they came to the banks of a river, which were well peopled, and yielded abundance of provisions of the country, and flocks of sheep.[5] The road is all made by hand, broad and well built, and, in some bad places, it is paved. Having arrived at the river, which is called Turicarami,[6] he formed his camp in a large village called Puechio,[7] and all the chiefs who lived on the lower course of the river came to the Governor to make their peace, while the inhabitants of the village came out to meet him. The Governor received them with much love, and informed them of the orders of his Majesty that they should know and be obedient to the church and to his Majesty. When they understood what was said, through interpreters, they replied that they desired to be his vassals, and that they would receive the Governor with the solemnity that might be required; so they served him and brought him provisions. Before reaching this place, at the distance of a flight from a cross-bow, there is a large place with a fortress surrounded by a wall, and many rooms inside, where the Christians lodged, that the Indians might not be affronted. On this occasion, as on all others when the Indians submitted peacefully, the Governor ordered, under severe penalties, "that no harm should be done to them either in person or goods, that none of their provisions should be taken, beyond those which they chose to give for the sustenance of the Christians, and he declared that those who acted differently should be

---

[5] So the first conquerors called the llamas and alpacas.

[6] This is the river Chira.

[7] See my translation of *Cieza de Leon*, p. 213. He calls the place *Pocheos*. Garcilasso de la Vega has *Puchiu*, ii, p. 424.

punished ;" for every day the Indians brought in all the
supplies that were wanted, as well as fodder for the horses,
and they did all the service that was required of them.

The Governor, seeing that the banks of that river were
fertile and well peopled, ordered search to be made in the
neighbourhood for a well sheltered port, and a very good one
was found on the sea-coast, near the valley ; and Caciques
or Lords of many vassals were found, in positions which
were convenient for them to come and do service on the
banks of the river. The Governor went to visit all these
villages, and the district appeared to him to be suitable for
a Spanish settlement. In order to comply with the commands of his Majesty, and that the natives might come to
be converted and to receive a knowledge of our Holy
Catholic Faith, he sent a messenger to the Spaniards who
had been left at Tumbez, ordering them to come that, with
the consent of all, a settlement might be formed on a site
most convenient for his Majesty's service, and for the good
of the natives. After he had sent this messenger, it oc-
curred to him that delay might arise unless a person went,
of whom the Caciques and Indians of Tumbez were in awe,
so that they might assist in the march of the Spaniards.
So he sent his brother Hernando Pizarro, Captain General.
Afterwards the Governor learnt that certain chiefs in the
hills would not submit, although they had received the
orders of his Majesty, so he sent a Captain with twenty-five
horse and foot, to reduce them to the service of his Majesty.
Finding that they had abandoned their villages, the Captain
sent to require them to come in peacefully, but they came
prepared for war, and the Captain came out against them.
In a short time many were killed and wounded, and they
were defeated. The Captain once more demanded that they
should submit, threatening that, if they refused, he would
destroy them. So they submitted, and the Captain received
them, and leaving all that province at peace, he returned to

the place where the Governor remained, bringing the chiefs
with him.   The Governor received them very kindly, and
ordered them to return to their villages, and to bring back
their people.   The Captain said that he had found mines
of fine gold in the hills round the villages of these chiefs,
and that the inhabitants collected it.   He brought specimens, and added that the mines were twenty leagues from
that town.

The Captain who went to Tumbez for the people, returned
with them in thirty days.   Some of them came by sea, with
the stores, in a ship, in a barque, and in balsas.   These
ships had come from Panama with merchandise, and brought
no troops, for the Captain Diego de Almagro remained
there, preparing a fleet, in which to come and form a settlement for himself.   As soon as the Governor heard that the
ships had arrived and landed the stores, he set out from the
village of Puechio, with some troops, to descend the river.
On reaching a place, where dwelt a chief named Lachira, he
found certain Christians who had landed.   They complained
to the Governor that the chief had ill-treated them, and that
fear had prevented them from sleeping during the previous
night, because they saw the Indians marching about under
arms.

The Governor made inquiries, and found that the chief of
Lachira and his principal men, with another chief, named Almotaxe,[8] had formed a conspiracy to kill the Christians on the
very day that the Governor arrived.   Having considered
the information, the Governor sent secretly to have the chief
Almotaxe and the principal men seized, while he himself
apprehended the chief of Lachira and some of his leading
men, who confessed their crime.   Then he ordered justice
to be executed, burning the Cacique of Almotaxe and his
head men, some Indians, and all the principal men of

    [8] I suspect this should be Amotape, a place on the river Chira, where
there are now some fine cotton estates.

Lachira. He did not execute justice upon the chief of Lachira, because his fault did not appear to be so great, and because, if he was killed, both the provinces would remain without a head, and would be lost. He was told that in future he must be true, and that the first treason would be his ruin. He was to govern all his own people, and also those of Almotaxe, until a boy, the heir of the lordship of Almotaxe, reached an age when he could be entrusted with the government.

This severity filled all the surrounding country with fear, insomuch that a confederacy which was said to have been formed to attack the Spaniards was dissolved; and from henceforth the Indians served better, and with more fear than before. Having executed this justice, and collected the people and stores which came from Tumbez, the Governor viewed the district, in concert with the Reverend Father Friar Vicente de Valverde, a monk of the order of San Domingo, and with the officers of his Majesty. In this region it was found that all necessaries for a place where Spaniards might settle were combined, that the natives were able to work without being overcome with fatigue, and that attention could be given to their conversion in accordance with the desire of his Majesty. The Governor, with the concurrence of his officers, therefore, established and founded a town in the name of his Majesty. Near the banks of the river, and six leagues from the sea port, there was a chief, the lord of a village, named Tangarara, to which the Spaniards gave the name of San Miguel.[9] In order that the ships which had come from Panama might receive no loss by delaying their return voyage, the Governor, with the concurrence of the officers of his Majesty, ordered certain gold, which had been presented by these chiefs and those of

[9] At first the city was built at Tangarara, in the Chira valley, but the site was abandoned on account of its unhealthiness. It is now in the valley of Piura. See my translation of *Cieza de Leon*, p. 213.

Tumbez, to be melted. A fifth was set apart as belonging to his Majesty. The rest, belonging to the company, was borrowed by the Governor from his troops, to be paid with the first gold they should obtain ; and with this gold the fleet was despatched, the freight was paid, and the merchants sent off their goods, and so they departed. The Governor sent to advise the Captain Almagro, his comrade, how much God and his Majesty would be injured if he attempted to form a new settlement. Having despatched the ships, the Governor divided the land amongst those who settled in the new town, for, without aid of the natives, they could neither have maintained nor peopled it. If the Caciques had been made to serve, without being assigned to persons who would be responsible, the natives would have suffered much injury ; for when the Spaniards know the Indians who are assigned to them, they treat them well, and take care of them. Influenced by these considerations, and with the approval of the monk and of officers, who thought that such a measure would be for the service of God and the good of the natives, the Governor assigned the Caciques and Indians to the settlers in this town, that they might assist in their maintenance, and that the Christians might teach them our holy Faith, in obedience to the orders of his Majesty that measures should be taken which were best for the service of God, of himself, and for the good of the country and of the natives. Alcaldes, Regidores, and other public officers were elected, who were given instructions by which they were to be guided.

The Governor received intelligence that the way to Chincha and Cuzco passed through very populous districts, which were rich and fertile, and that there was an inhabited valley called Caxamalca,[1] ten or twelve days' journey from his settlement, where Atabaliba[2] resided, who was the

---

[1] Cassa-marca ; from *cassa* snow and *marca* a village.

[2] Atahuallpa.

THE VALLEY OF PIURA.

greatest lord among these natives, whom they all obeyed, and who had conquered lands far distant from the country of his birth. When he came to the province of Caxamalca, he found it to be so rich and pleasant that he settled there, and continued to conquer other lands from thence. This lord is held in so much dread that the natives of the valley are not so reconciled to the service of his Majesty as would otherwise be the case, but they rather favour Atabaliba and say that they acknowledge him as their lord and no other, and that a small detachment from his army would suffice to kill all the Christians. For the Indians excite great terror by their accustomed cruelty. The Governor resolved to march in search of Atabaliba, to reduce him to the service of his Majesty, and to pacify the surrounding provinces. For when he was once conquered the rest would soon be reduced to submission.

The Governor departed from the city of San Miguel,[3] in search of Atabaliba, on the 24th of September, 1532, and on the first day his troops crossed the river on two rafts, the horses swimming. That night he slept at a village on the other side of the river. After three more days he arrived at the valley of Piura, and came to a fortress belonging to a chief, where they met a Captain with some Spaniards, who had been sent to subdue that chief, in order to relieve the Chief of San Miguel. The Governor remained there for ten days, making preparations for the march. On mustering the Christians he intended to take with him, he found he had sixty-seven horse and one hundred and ten foot soldiers, three of them with guns, and some with cross-bows. The Lieutenant in charge of San Miguel wrote to report that few Christians remained there, so the Governor proclaimed that " those who wished to return and settle in the town of San Miguel would have Indians assigned to

[3] Antonio Navarro, the Accountant, was left in command at San Miguel ; and the Royal Treasurer Riquelme remained with him.

maintain them, like the other settlers who remained there, and that he would proceed with his conquest with those that were left, whether they were few or many." Five horsemen and four foot soldiers returned; so that, with these, there were fifty-five settlers, besides ten or twelve others who remained by their own wish, without citizenship. The Governor then mustered sixty-two horsemen and one hundred and two foot soldiers. He ordered that arms should be prepared for those who had none, both for their persons and horses, and he re-organised the cross-bow men, completing their number to twenty, and appointing a captain to take charge of them.

Having made all necessary arrangements, he set out with his troops, and, after marching until noon, he arrived at a large court, surrounded by walls, belonging to a chief named Pabor. The Governor and his troops lodged there. He learnt that this chief had been ruined, for that the old Cuzco, father of Atabaliba, had destroyed twenty villages and killed their inhabitants. But, in spite of this injury, the chief had many vassals, and bordering on his territory was that of his brother, who was as great a lord as himself. These natives submitted peacefully, and were assigned to the city of San Miguel. This settlement, and that of Piura, are in very fertile level valleys. The Governor here obtained tidings of the neighbouring chiefs, and of the road to Caxamalca, and he was informed that further on there was a great town, called Caxas, in which there was a garrison of Atabaliba, waiting for the Christians, in case they should come that way. This being known to the Governor, he sent a Captain[4] secretly, with horse and foot, to the town of Caxas,[5] with orders that, if the enemy wished to oppose their passage with violence, he was to strive to inspire them with peaceful

[4] This was Hernando de Soto.

[5] Across the Andes, on the Marañon watershed. See my translation of *Cieza de Leon*, p. 209.

feelings, and to bring them into the service of his Majesty. On that day the Captain departed. The next day the Governor set out, and reached a town called Çaran,[6] where he waited for the Captain who had gone to Caxas. The chief of the town brought the Governor supplies of sheep and other things, to a fortress at which the Governor arrived at noon. Next day he left the fortress and came to the town of Çaran, where he ordered his camp to be formed, to wait for the Captain who had gone to Caxas. After five days the Captain sent a messenger to the Governor, with news that he had succeeded. The Governor presently replied from the village where he was waiting, that, after he had completed his work, he should join him, and, on the road, visit and reduce another town near that of Caxas, called Gicabamba;[7] and that it was reported that the chief of Zaran was lord over rich villages, and of a fertile valley, which was assigned to the settlers of the city of San Miguel. During the eight days that the Governor was waiting for the Captain, the Spaniards were re-organised, and the horses were refreshed for the coming journey. When the Captain returned with his troops, he gave an account to the Governor of what he had seen in those villages. He said that it had taken him two days and one night to reach Caxas, without resting, except for meals. Even then they would not have arrived (though they had good guides) if they had not met some spies from the village, some of whom they captured, and from whom they obtained information. Having put his men in order, the Captain followed the road until he reached the village, and at the entrance he found a royal building, where there were traces of armed men. The village of Caxas is in a small valley surrounded by mountains. The people were in a commotion, but the Captain pacified them, and gave them to understand that he came, on the part of the Governor, to receive their submission as vassals of

[6] Zaran, still in the Piura valley.   [7] Huanca-pampa.

the Emperor.   Then a chief came out and said that he was
in the service of Atabaliba, receiving tribute from these
villages.   He described the road to Caxamalca, and mentioned the intention of Atabaliba to visit the Christians.
He spoke of the city of Cuzco, thirty days' journey from
Caxas, which is a league round, and the house of the Cacique
is four cross-bow shots in length.   There is also a hall,
where is the dead body of old Cuzco,[8] the floor of which is
plated with silver, and the roof and walls with gold and
silver interwoven.   He added that it was a year since the
Cuzco,[9] son of old Cuzco, lost those villages, when they
were taken by his brother Atabaliba, who rebelled and conquered the land, exacting great tribute, and daily perpetrat-
ing cruelties.   For they not only have to give their goods
as tribute, but also their sons and daughters.   The royal
building was reported to belong to Atabaliba, who, a few
days before, had gone hence, with a part of his army.   They
found a great and strong building in that town of Caxas,
surrounded by a mud wall with doorways, in which there
were many women spinning and weaving cloth for the army
of Atabaliba; and there were no men with them, except the
porters who guarded them.   At the entrance of the village
there were certain Indians hung up by the feet; and this
chief stated that Atabaliba had ordered them to be killed,
because one of them entered the house of the women to
sleep with one; who, with all the porters who consented to
his entering the house, was hanged.

As soon as this Captain had pacified the village of Caxas,
he marched to Guacamba,[1] which is distant one day's journey,
and is larger than Caxas, containing finer edifices, and a
fortress built entirely of cut stones, the larger stones being
of five or six *palmos*, and so closely joined that there ap-

---

[8] Ynca Huayna Ccapac.   [9] Huascar Ynca.
[1] Huanca-pampa, on a river of the same name, flowing into the
Marañon.

peared to be no mortar between them. There was a lofty masonry platform, with two flights of stone steps, between two buildings. A small river flows through this town, and by that of Caxas, which supplies them with water, and over which they have bridges with very good pavements. A broad road, made by hands, connects these two towns ; and the same road traverses all that land from Cuzco to Quito, a distance of more than three hundred leagues.[2] The road is level, and the part which traverses the mountains is very well made, being broad enough for six men on horseback to ride abreast. By the side of the road flow channels of water brought from a distance, at which the travellers can drink. At the end of each day's journey there is a house, like an inn, where those who go and come, can lodge. At the entrance to this road, from the town of Caxas, there was a house at the head of a bridge, where a guard was stationed to receive transit dues in kind, from those who came and went; and no man could take a load out of the town without paying the toll. This was an ancient custom, and Atabaliba suspended it, in so far as it affected the things that were brought for his troops. No passenger could enter or depart with a load by any other road than that on which the guard was stationed, on pain of death.

He also said that he found, in these two towns, two houses full of shoes, cakes of salt, a food like *albondigas*,[3] and other

---

[2] " In the long day's journey from the syenitic rocks of Zaulaca to the valley of San Felipe (rich in fossils, and situated at the foot of the icy Paramo of Yamoca) we were obliged to wade through the Rio de Guancabamba (which flows into the Amazons) no less than twenty-seven times, on account of the windings of the stream ; while we continually saw near us, running in a straight line along the side of a steep precipice, the remains of the high-built road of the Incas, with its Tambos." (*Aspects of Nature*, ii, p. 277.) Humboldt further mentions that the Guancabamba, in the lower part of its course, is made to serve as a route for a swimming post to Jaen de Bracamoros.

[3] Balls of forced meat chopped small, with eggs and spice. A Spanish

stores for the use of the troops of Atabaliba. He added
that these towns were well ruled, and that the people lived
in an orderly manner. A principal Indian and some others
came with the Captain. The Captain said that this Indian
had come with presents for the Governor. This messenger
said to the Governor that his lord Atabaliba had sent him
from Caxamalca to bring the present, which consisted of
two fountains made of stone, like fortresses, and used to
drink out of, and two loads of dried geese, skinned and
prepared to be powdered and used for fumigating; for such
is the custom of the lords of that land. The messenger[4]
told the Governor that he had been instructed to say that
Atabaliba desired to be his friend, and that he was waiting
to receive him in peace at Caxamalca. The Governor received the present, and spoke to the messenger, saying
that he rejoiced greatly at his arrival, being a messenger
from Atabaliba, whom he desired to see by reason of the
things that he had heard of him ; that, as he knew that
Atabaliba was making war upon his enemies, he had resolved to go and see him, and be his friend and brother,
aiding him in his conquests with the Christians who accompanied him. He ordered that food should be given to the
messenger, and to those who came with him, and that they
should have all that they needed and be well lodged as the
ambassadors of so great a lord. After they were rested, he
ordered them to be brought before him, and said that they
were to do as they pleased, either to depart at once or to
rest for another day. The messenger replied that he desired

dish. Martinez Molino, the celebrated cook of Philip III, in his treatise
on cookery published at Madrid in 1617, enumerates a great variety of
albondigas.

[4] This was Titu Atauchi, the brother of Atahuallpa, according to
Garcilasso. (Pt. II, lib. i, cap. 17.) He brought many other presents :
sheep, deer, birds, maize, dried fruits, honey, pepper, cloths, vases of
gold and silver, emeralds, and bracelets called *chipana.*

to return with the answer to his lord. The Governor then said—" Repeat what I have already told you, that I will not stop at any village on the road, that I may quickly arrive and see your lord." He gave the messenger a shirt, and other things from Castille, to take with him. After the departure of the messenger, the Governor rested for another two days because the troops that had come from Caxas were fatigued with their journey. In this interval he wrote to the citizens of San Miguel and gave them an account of the land and of the news from Atabaliba; and he sent them the two vases in the form of fortresses, and cloth of the country from Caxas. It is wonderful how highly this cloth is prized in Spain for its workmanship. It is looked upon more as silk than as wool.[5] The cloths are enriched with many patterns and figures in beaten gold, very well embroidered. As soon as the Governor had despatched his messengers to the town of San Miguel, he set out, and marched for three days without finding a village or any water, except at one small spring where it could only be got at with difficulty.[6] At the end of three days he arrived at a large walled enclosure where no inhabitants were found. It proved to belong to the Lord of a village called Copiz, in an adjacent valley, and that fortress was abandoned because there was no water. Next morning the Governor started very early, because it was a long march to the inhabited valley. At noon he reached a house with a surrounding wall, containing very good lodgings, where some Indians came out to receive him. But there were neither provisions nor water, so the Governor advanced two leagues further, to the village of the chief. Having arrived, he ordered that the troops should be lodged together, in a certain part of the village. He was informed by the prin-

---

[5] Made from the soft vicuña fleeces.
[6] He was crossing the vast sandy desert of Sechura.

cipal Indian of the place, which was called Motux,[7] that the chief was in Caxamalca, and that he had gone there with three hundred men of war. The Governor found there a Captain appointed by Atabaliba. The Spaniards rested at Motux for four days, and, during that time, the Governor saw some portion of the inhabited country belonging to the chief, which appeared to be extensive, and to include a fertile valley. All the villages between this place and the city of San Miguel are in valleys, as well as all those of which he had received information, as far as the foot of the mountains near Caxamalca. On this road all the people have the same manner of living. The women wear a long robe which reaches to the ground, like the dresses of women in Castille. The men have short shirts. These people are dirty. They eat flesh and fish all raw, and maize boiled and toasted. They have other filthy things in the way of sacrifices and mosques,[8] which they hold in veneration, and they offer up to them the best of all that they have. Each month they sacrifice their own children, and with the blood they anoint the faces of the idols, and the doors of the mosques. They do this on the sepulchres of the dead, and the victims who are sacrificed, go willingly to their deaths, laughing, dancing, and singing. After they have drunk well, they themselves ask that their heads may be cut off. They also sacrifice sheep. The mosques are different from the other houses. They are surrounded by very well-built walls, in the highest part of the town. In Tumbez they wear the same clothes and perform the same

[7] This is a misprint for Motupe, a rich and fertile valley. Lorente identifies it with Motupe. (*Hist. del Peru*, ii, p. 120.) Zarate gives the word correctly as Motupe, not Motux. (*Zarate*, lib. ii, cap. iii, p. 20.) It is the Mutupi of Garcilasso de la Vega, ii, p. 424.

[8] Xeres always gives the name of *mosques* to the temples of the Peruvians. The fathers of the Spanish conquerors had served in the campaign of Granada, and their minds were full of the things relating to the Moorish infidels.

sacrifices as in these villages. They sow the crops in the
level ground on the banks of the rivers, distributing water
through channels. They grow much maize, and other seeds
and roots which they eat. In that land there is little rain.

During two days the Governor marched through well-
peopled valleys,[9] sleeping at the end of each journey in
houses surrounded by walls. The lords of the villages say
that the old Cuzco[1] lodged in these houses when he travelled
by this road. The people of the country received the
Governor in peace. On another day he travelled over a dry
and sandy tract until he reached another well-peopled valley,
through which a great and rapid river flowed.[2] The river
was much swollen, so the Governor passed the night on the
hither side, and ordered a Captain to swim across it, with
some others who knew how to swim, and to occupy the villages on the other side, thus preventing any people from
disturbing the passage. The Captain Hernando Pizarro
swam across, and the people of a village on the other side
received him in peace, and lodged him in a walled fortress.
But as he saw that all the Indians of the villages were in
arms, though a few had been friendly, he asked them
touching Atabaliba, and whether he was waiting for the
Christians with pacific or warlike intentions. None of the
Indians wished to tell the truth, by reason of the fear they
had of Atabaliba; until one of the principal men among
them was taken apart and tortured. He then said that
Atabaliba waited with hostile intentions, his army being in
three detachments, one at the foot of the mountains, another

[9] The valleys of the rivers of Motupe and Leche.

[1] Xeres never seems to have heard the word Ynca. He calls the
Ynca Huayna Ccapac, the father of Atahuallpa and Huascar, by the
name of " Old Cuzco" throughout ; mistaking the name of the capital
city for the name of the sovereign. He also calls Huascar " Young
Cuzco". Hernando Pizarro makes the same mistake.

[2] This was the valley of Cinto. See *Cieza de Leon*, p. 240. Lorente
identifies the river with that of *Leche*.

on the summit, and another at Caxamalca. He also told
them that Atabaliba waited in great pride, saying that he
would kill the Christians, whom he hated. The next
morning the Captain sent this news to the Governor. Then
the Governor ordered trees to be cut down on both sides of
the river, on which the troops and baggage might pass.
Three rafts were constructed, on which the men continued
to cross over during the whole day, the horses swimming.
In all this the Governor worked hard, until the army had
crossed. He then went over, and lodged in the fortress
where the Captain was. He sent for a Chief, from whom
he learnt that Atabaliba was on the other side of Caxamalca,
in Guamachuco, with many warriors, his force numbering
fifty thousand men. When the Governor heard of so large a
number, believing that the Chief had made a mistake in his
account, he was told how the Indians counted, from one to
ten, from ten to a hundred, from ten hundreds making a
thousand; and that five tens of thousands were the numbers
which Atabaliba had with him. The Chief who gave the
Governor this information was the principal Chief among
those of that river. He said that when Atabaliba visited
his country he had concealed himself from fear; and when
Atabaliba could not find him in his village he killed, out of
five thousand inhabitants, as many as four thousand, and
took six hundred women and six hundred boys to distribute
them among his soldiers. The Chief of that village and
fortress where the Governor lodged, was called Cinto,[3] and
he was then with Atabaliba.

Here the Governor and his troops rested during four
days, and on the day before he departed, he spoke with a
principal Indian of the province of San Miguel, and said to
him : "Are you bold enough to go to Caxamalca as a spy,
and to bring me news of what is going on there?" The

---

[3] The valley itself was called Cinto. Garcilasso de la Vega has *Cintu*,
ii, p. 424.

Indian answered : " I will not go as a spy, but I will go as
your messenger to speak with Atabaliba, and I will learn
whether there are warriors in the mountains, and the intentions of Atabaliba." The Governor said : " Go as you desire,
and if there are troops in the mountains (as is reported here),
send me word by one of the Indians whom you take with
you.   Speak with Atabaliba and his people, and tell him of
the kind treatment that I and the Christians show to the
friendly chiefs, that we only make war upon those who
attack us, and that all you have said is true, and according
to what you have seen.   If Atabaliba wishes to be friendly,
tell him that I will be his friend and brother, and will favour
and help him in his war."   That Indian departed on the
embassy, while the Governor continued his march across
those valleys, arriving every day at a village with a walled
house like a fortress.   After three days he reached a village
at the foot of the mountains,[4] leaving the road along which
he had hitherto marched, on his right hand, for it leads by
the way of those valleys to Chincha.   The other road goes
direct to Caxamalca.   The road to Chincha passed through
many villages, and led from the river of San Miguel.   It
was paved, and bounded on each side by a wall.   Two carts
could be driven abreast upon it.   From Chincha it led to
Cuzco, and, in many parts of it, rows of trees were planted
on either side, for the sake of their shade on the road.
This road was made for old Cuzco, when he visited his do-
minions, and those houses, surrounded by walls, were his
lodgings.   Some of the Christians were of opinion that the

---

[4] Hernando Pizarro calls this place *La Ramada*.   It is in the valley
of the river Jequetepeque, at the foot of the Andes.   By the route across
the Andes followed by Pizarro, the new railway now under construction
will pass.   Its terminus on the coast is at Pacasmayo, and it is taken up
the valley of Jequetepeque, by San Pedro, Guadaloupe, and Magdalena,
and over the Andes, to Caxamarca.   From Magdalena another road
branches off, and passes down the valley of Chicama to Truxillo.   This
was the route taken by Lieutenant Maw in 1829.

Governor should take this road to Chincha, because there was a difficult mountain to traverse by the other road before reaching Caxamalca, in which the soldiers of Atabaliba were posted, and some disaster might befall, if that road was taken. The Governor answered that " they now had news of Atabaliba, and that they had been marching in search of him ever since they left the river of San Miguel. If they turned aside now, the Indians would say that it was from fear, and they would become more proud than they were before." For these and other reasons the Governor said that he would not turn aside from his intention of marching to the place where Atabaliba was, wherever that might be. He exhorted all his men to make up their minds to act as he hoped they would, and to have no fear of the great number of soldiers in the army of Atabaliba, for though the Christians might be few, yet the help of our Lord would be sufficient to confound their enemies, and to make them come to a knowledge of our Holy Catholic Faith. He reminded them that every day they had seen our Lord work a miracle for them in their need, and he assured them that He would be with them still, seeing that they went with the good intention of bringing these infidels to a knowledge of the truth, without doing harm or injury to any except those who desired to show opposition and who appeared in arms.

After the Governor had made this speech, all declared that he should take the road which seemed best to him, and that they would follow cheerfully, and show him what each man could do when the time came.

Having arrived at the foot of the mountains they rested for a day to arrange the order for the ascent. The Governor, after taking counsel with experienced officers, resolved to leave the rear guard and baggage, taking with him forty horse and sixty foot. He entrusted the remainder to the care of a Captain, and ordered him to follow with much circumspection, telling him that he would receive instructions as to what he was to do. Having made these arrangements, the Governor commenced the ascent. The horsemen led their horses up until, at noon, they reached a pallisaded fort on the top of a hill, in a narrow part of the road where, with few Christians, the way might be made good against a great army. It was so steep that, in places, they had to ascend by steps, and there was no other place but the road by which the ascent could be effected. This pass was ascended without its being defended by anyone. The fortress was surrounded by stone walls, and was built on a hill with declivitous rocks on all sides. Here the Governor stopped to rest and have some food. The cold is so great on these mountains that some of the horses, accustomed to the warmth of the valleys, were frost-bitten. Thence the Governor went to sleep at a village, and sent a messenger to the forces in his rear, with the news that they might safely advance through the pass, and with orders that they were to push on, so as to pass the night at the fortress. The Governor lodged that night at a village, in a strong house surrounded by a masonry wall, as extensive as a fort of Spain, with its doorways. If the people had had the artists and tools of Spain, this surrounding wall could not have been better built. The people of this village had taken up arms, except some women and a few Indians. The Governor ordered a Captain to take two from amongst the Indians, and to examine each separately touching the affairs of that land, asking them where Atabaliba was, and if he intended peace or war. The Captain learnt from them that Atabaliba had reached Caxamalca three days before, with a large force; but they knew nothing of his intentions. They said, however, that thay had always heard that Atabaliba wished to have peace with the Christians. The people of the village were on his side. Towards sunset one of the Indians who had gone with the messenger arrived, and said that he had been sent back by his master when he was near

Caxamalca, because he had encountered two messengers of Atabaliba who were coming behind him and would arrive next day. He reported that Atabaliba was at Caxamalca, and that there were no armed men on the road. The Governor sent back this intelligence to the Captain in charge of the baggage, by a letter, in which he was told that the Governor would make but a short march next day, in order that the Captain might join him, and that the whole force would then advance together. The next morning the Governor marched with his troops, still ascending the mountains, and stopped on a plain on the summit, near some springs of water, to wait for those who were still behind. The Spaniards rested in the cotton tents they brought with them, making fires to protect themselves from the cold of the mountains. For on the plains of Castille it is not colder than on these heights, which are clear of trees, but covered with a grass,[5] like short *esparto*.[6] There are a few stunted trees, and the water is so cold that it cannot be drunk without being first warmed. After the Governor had rested here for a short time, the rear guard arrived, and also the messengers sent by Atabaliba, who brought ten sheep. Being brought before the Governor, and having made their obeisances, they said :—" Atabaliba has sent these sheep for the Christians, and he would know the day on which they will arrive at Caxamalca, that he may send out provisions on the road." The Governor received them well, and said that he rejoiced at their arrival with a message from his brother Atabaliba, and that he would come as quickly as possible. After they had eaten food, and had some rest, the Governor questioned the messengers touching the affairs of their land, and respecting the wars waged by Atabaliba. One of them answered that Atabaliba had been five days in Caxamalca, waiting for the Governor, and that he had only

---

[5] This grass is the *Stipa Ychu*. It grows in large coarse tufts.

[6] *Esparto* is feather grass, also a *Stipa*.

a few troops with him, the rest having been sent to make war against his brother Cuzco.[7] The Governor then asked what had taken place in all those wars, and how Atabaliba had commenced his conquests. The Indian answered:— "My Lord Atabaliba is the son of old Cuzco,[8] who is now dead, but who once ruled over all these lands. He left to his son Atabaliba the dominion over a great province called Quito; and to another elder son he left all the other lands and the principal lordship, and, as successor to the sovereignty, he was called Cuzco, like his father. But, not content with the sovereignty, he came to wage war on his brother Atabaliba, who sent him messages, beseeching him to allow him to enjoy peacefully the inheritance that had been left him by his father. But the Cuzco would not, and he killed his heirs, and a brother of both of them, who came with the message. Seeing this, Atabaliba came against him with a large army, as far as a province called Tumipomba,[9] which was within the territory of his brother; and, because the people resisted, he burnt their town and killed them all. Thence the news came to his brother that he had invaded the land, and was advancing against him. When the Cuzco heard this, he fled to his own land, and Atabaliba marched onwards, conquering the lands of the Cuzco, without meeting any resistance, because the people had heard of the punishment he had inflicted upon Tumipomba. He obtained recruits from all the lands he conquered, and when he arrived at Caxamalca, the place appeared to be in a fertile land, so he rested there while all the other territory of his brother was subdued. He sent a captain with two thousand men against the city where his brother lived, and as his brother had a vast army, all these men were killed. Ata-

---

[7] The Ynca Huascar.   [8] The Ynca Huayna Ccapac.

[9] A corruption of Tumi-pampa; a place in the kingdom of Quito. Huayna Ccapac built a magnificent palace there, which was his favourite residence.

baliba then sent more troops under two captains, and in two
months tidings came that these two captains had gained all
the lands of the Cuzco, had arrived at his city, defeated his
army, taken him prisoner, and seized much gold and silver."
The Governor said to the messenger :—"I rejoice at the
tidings you have given me, and at the victory of your Lord;
for his brother, not content with what he had, strove to reduce under his yoke the Lord who had received his inheritance from his father.   To the proud it happens as it has
done to this Cuzco : for they not only fail to get what they
unjustly grasp at, but remain with the loss of their own
property and freedom."   The Governor, believing that all that
this Indian had told him, on the part of Atabaliba, was intended to amaze the Christians, and make them understand
his power and skill, also said to the messenger:—"I well believe that what you have told me is true, because Atabaliba
is a great Lord, and I am informed that he is a good soldier.
Yet I would have you to know that my Lord the Emperor,
who is King of Spain and of all the Indies and of Tierra
Firme, and Lord over all the World, has many servants who
are greater Lords than Atabaliba, and his captains have
fought and taken much greater Lords than either Atabaliba,
his brother, or his father.   The Emperor has sent me to
these lands to bring the inhabitants to a knowledge of God,
and, in his service, I have defeated greater Lords than
Atabaliba, with these few Christians that are with me now.
If he should wish for my friendship, and to receive me
peacefully, as other Lords have done, I shall be his good
friend, and I will assist him in his conquest, leaving him in
his present state ; for I go through these lands to discover
the other sea.   But if he should wish for war, I will make
war, as I have done against the chief of the island of Santiago, and against the chief of Tumbez, and against all
others who have wished to have war with me.   I make war
upon no one, nor do I molest any one, unless war is made
upon me."

When the messengers heard these things, they were at first so astounded that they could not speak, to think that so few Spaniards could have performed such wonderful things. After a time they expressed a wish to go with this reply to their Lord, and to tell him that the Christians would come quickly, in order that he might send out provisions on the road. The Governor dismissed them. The next morning he continued the march, still over the mountains, and that night he slept at some villages he came to, in a valley. As soon as the Governor arrived, there came the chief messenger, whom Atabaliba had first sent with the present of the fountains like fortresses, and who came to Çaran by way of Caxas. The Governor was very glad to see him, and inquired after Atabaliba. The messenger answered that he was well, and that he had sent ten sheep for the Christians. He spoke very freely, and, from his conversation, he seemed to be an intelligent man.

When he had completed his speech, the Governor asked the interpreters what he had said. They answered that he had repeated the same as had been said by the other messengers the day before; but that he had added many arguments, praising the greatness of his Lord and the vast power of his army, and assuring the Governor that Atabaliba would receive him in peace, and that he desired to have him as a friend and a brother. The Governor answered with fair words, such as the other had used. This ambassador was served as a Lord, and had five or six cups of fine gold, from which he drank, and he gave the Spaniards *chicha*[1] to drink out of them, which he brought with him. He said that he desired to go to Caxamalca with the Governor.

Next morning the Governor started, his way leading over the mountains as before, and he reached a village of Atabaliba, where he rested for one day. Next day the messenger

---

[1] Fermented liquor made from maize. The correct Quichua word is *acca*.

came in whom the Governor had sent to Atabaliba. He
was one of the principal Indians of the province of San
Miguel. When he saw the messenger of Atabaliba, who
was present, he rushed upon him, and seized hold of his
ears, pulling them fiercely until the Governor ordered him
to let go, for if they had been left alone mischief would
have come of it. The Governor said to him, " Why have
you done this to the messenger of my brother Atabaliba ?"
He answered, "This is a great rogue, this carrier of Atabaliba. He comes here to tell lies, pretending to be a great
man. Atabaliba is in warlike array outside Caxamalca on
the plain. He has a large army, and I found the town
empty. I went thence to the camp, and saw many people
and flocks, and a quantity of tents, and all was ready for
war. They wanted to kill me, only it was said that if I
was killed, their ambassadors, who are here, would also be
put to death, and that they would not be allowed to go
until I returned. They would give me no food without
bartering. I asked them to let me see Atabaliba and deliver my message, but they refused, saying that he was
fasting, and could not speak to any one. An uncle of his
came out to speak to me, and I told him that I was your
messenger, and that I was ready to tell him anything he
chose to ask. He inquired of me what sort of people were
the Christians, and what kind of arms they bore. I replied
that they were valiant men and great warriors, that they
had horses which ran like the wind, and that those who rode
them carried long lances, with which they killed as many
people as they met, overtaking them in two jumps, while
the horses killed many with their feet and mouths. I added
that the Christians who marched on foot were very alert,
carrying on one arm a shield of wood with which they defended themselves, and strong tunics quilted with cotton ;
that they had very sharp swords with which they cut a man
in two at each blow, and that with these they could cut all

the arms used by the Indians.   Others, I said, carry slings
with which they shoot from afar, and at every shot they
kill a man.   Others shoot with powder, sending forth lumps
of powder, which kill many men.   They answered that all
this was nought, that the Christians were few in number,
that the horses had no arms, and that they would soon kill
them with their lances.   I replied that the horses had thick
skins which their lances could not penetrate.   They then
said that they did not fear the two shots of fire, and that
the Christians only had two.   When I wished to depart,
I asked them to let me see Atabaliba, as his messengers
came and spoke to the Governor, who was better than he,
but they would not let me see him, and so I departed.   See
then if I have not good reason for killing this man; for,
being a carrier of Atabaliba (as they have told me that he
is), he speaks with you, and eats at your table, while I, who
am a Chief, was not allowed to speak with Atabaliba, nor
would they give me to eat, and it was only by good arguments that they were induced to refrain from killing me."
The messenger of Atabaliba replied with some fear, seeing
that the old Indian had spoken so boldly.   He said, " If
there were no people in the town of Caxamalca, it was to
leave the houses empty for the reception of the Christians,
and Atabaliba is in the field because such is his custom
after he has commenced a war.   If they would not allow
the messenger to speak to him, it was because he was fasting, according to the custom, and he could see no one by
reason of being in retirement, at which time he speaks to
no one.   No one dared to tell him that the messenger was
waiting, but if he had known it he would have made him
come in, and would have given him food."   He used many
other arguments to show that the intentions of Atabaliba
were friendly.   If all the conversations between this Indian
and the Governor were written down in full, it would fill a
large book; so, for the sake of brevity, a summary of them

is given. The Governor said that he well believed it was
as the Indian stated, and that he had no less confidence in
his brother Atabaliba. He continued to treat the man as
well as before, rebuking his own messenger, and telling
the ambassador that he regretted the ill treatment he had
received in his presence. But in secret he looked upon it
as certain that what his own messenger had told him was
true, by reason of the knowledge he had of the cautious
intrigues of the Indians.

Next day the Governor departed, and slept on a plain,
intending to reach Caxamalca at noon the day after, as they
told him it was near. Here messengers arrived from Atabaliba, with food for the Christians. Early next morning
the Governor started, with his troops in order of battle, and
marched to within a league of Caxamalca. Here he waited
for his rear guard to join him. All the troops got their
arms ready, and the Governor formed the Spaniards, horse
and foot, three deep, to enter the town. In this order the
Governor advanced, sending messengers to Atabaliba, that
he might come and meet him at the town of Caxamalca.
On reaching the entrance to Caxamalca, they saw the camp
of Atabaliba at a distance of a league, in the skirts of the
mountains. The Governor arrived at this town of Caxamalca on Friday, the 15th of November, 1532, at the hour
of vespers. In the middle of the town there is a great open
space,[2] surrounded by walls and houses. The Governor
occupied this position, and sent a messenger to Atabaliba,
to announce his arrival, to arrange a meeting, and that he
might show him where to lodge. Meanwhile he ordered
the town to be examined, with a view to discovering a
stronger position where he might pitch the camp. He
ordered all the troops to be stationed in the open space, and
the cavalry to remain mounted, until it was seen whether
Atabaliba would come. After examining the town it was

[2] Hernando Pizarro says that it was triangular.

found that there was no better position in the neighbourhood. This town, which is the principal place in the valley,
is situated on the skirts of a mountain, and there is a league
of open plain in front of it. Two rivers flow through the
valley, which is level, and well peopled, and surrounded by
mountains.[3] The town had two thousand inhabitants. At
its entrance there were two bridges, because two rivers flow
past. The *plaza* is larger than any in Spain, surrounded
by a wall, and entered by two doorways which open upon
the streets of the town. The houses are more than two
hundred paces in length, and very well built, being surrounded by strong walls, three times the height of a man.
The roofs are covered with straw and wood, resting on the
walls. The interiors are divided into eight rooms, much
better built than any we had seen before. Their walls are
of very well cut stones, and each lodging is surrounded by
its masonry wall with doorways, and has its fountain of
water in an open court, conveyed from a distance by pipes,
for the supply of the house. In front of the *plaza*, towards
the open country, a stone fortress is connected with it by a
staircase leading from the square to the fort. Towards the
open country there is another small door, with a narrow
staircase, all within the outer wall of the *plaza*. Above the
town, on the mountain side, where the houses commence,
there is another fort on a hill, the greater part of which is
hewn out of the rock. This is larger than the other, and
surrounded by three walls, rising spirally. They are of a
strength such as had not before been seen among the Indians.
Between the mountain and the great open space there is
another smaller court, entirely surrounded by buildings, in

    [3] Humboldt describes the fertile valley of Caxamarca as of an oval
shape, covering ninety-six to a hundred and twelve square miles, with a
small river winding through it. The soil is fertile, and the plain full of
cultivated fields and gardens, traversed by avenues of willows, large
flowered daturas, mimosas, and the beautiful *quenuar* trees (*Polylepis
villosa.*)

which there were many women for the service of Atabaliba.[4]
Before entering this city there is a house built in a court
surrounded by walls.   In the court there is a grove of trees
planted by hand.   They say that this is the house of the
Sun, for in each village they build their mosques to the
Sun.   There are many other mosques in this town, and they
hold them in veneration throughout the land.   When they
enter them, they take off their shoes at the doors.   The
people of all the villages we came to after ascending the
mountains, are superior to those we left behind.   Those of
the mountains are clean and more intelligent, and the women
are very modest.   The women wear over their clothes
highly ornamented girdles, fastened round the middle.
Over the gown they wear a mantle reaching from the head
to half down the legs, which is like the *mantilla* of Spain.
The men dress in shirts without sleeves, and outer mantles.
They all weave wool and cotton in their houses, and make
the cloth they require, and shoes for the men, of wool and
cotton.   The Governor was a long time in the plaza with his
men, waiting for Atabaliba either to come or to assign him
a lodging.   As it was getting late he sent a Captain[5] with
twenty horse to speak with Atabaliba, and to say that he
should come and confer with the Governor.   The Captain
had orders to preserve peace, and to pick no quarrel, even
if his men were provoked ; but to do his best to obtain a

---

[4] Humboldt states that the palace of the Ynca, at Cassa-marca, was
situated on a hill of porphyry which had originally been hollowed at the
surface, so that it surrounds the principal dwelling almost like a wall or
rampart.   A State prison and a municipal building (*Casa del Cabildo*)
have been erected on part of the ruins.   The ruins consist of fine cut
blocks of stone, two or three feet long, and placed upon each other
without cement.   There were steps cut in the rock, and minor buildings
for servants, partly of cut stones with sloped roofs, and partly of bricks
with vaulted recesses.

Humboldt made acquaintance, at Cassa-marca, with a family descended from Atahualpa, through females, called Astorpilco.

[5] This was Hernando de Soto.

hearing and return with the reply. This Captain had got
half-way, when the Governor went up into the fort, and saw
a great body of men in front of the tents. In order that the
Christians who had gone might be in no danger if they were
attacked, and be able to retreat from among the Indians
and defend themselves, he sent another Captain, his own
brother,[6] with other twenty horsemen, giving him orders
not to permit them to raise any shouts. In a little while it
began to rain and hail, and the Governor ordered the
Christians to take shelter in the rooms of the palace, and
the Captain of artillery, with his guns,[7] to station himself
and his men in the fortress. While they were there, an
Indian arrived from Atabaliba to tell the Governor that he
might lodge where he pleased, but not to go up into the fortress of the *plaza* ; and to excuse himself from coming on
the ground that he was fasting. The Governor replied
that he would do so, and that he had sent his brother to ask
for an interview, as he had a great desire to see and know
one of whom he had heard so much. The messenger went
back with this answer, and the Captain Hernando Pizarro
returned after nightfall with the Christians. On coming before the Governor they said that they had found a bad part
of the road, in a swamp, which had previously appeared to
be paved. For there is a broad road leading from the
town, made with earth and stone, as far as the camp of
Atabaliba. This pavement led over the bad places, but
they had broken it up at the swamp ; so that the Christians
had to pass by another way. They crossed two rivers
before reaching the camp. In front of it there is a river,
which the Indians cross by a bridge, and here is the camp,
surrounded by water. The Captain who went first left his
men on this side the river, that the Indians might not be

6 Hernando Pizarro.
7 The captain of artillery was Pedro de Candia, the stout-hearted
Greek. Their artillery consisted of two falconets.

excited, and he would not go by the bridge, fearing for his horse, so he crossed by the water, taking an interpreter with him. He passed through a squadron of infantry, and came to the lodging of Atabaliba, where there were four hundred Indians in an open space, who appeared to be a body guard. The tyrant was at the door of his lodging, sitting on a low stool, with many Indians before him, and women at his feet, who almost surrounded him.[8] He wore across his forehead a woollen fringe,[9] which looked like silk, of a crimson colour, fastened to the head by cords, so as to come down to the eyes, which made him look much graver than he really is. His eyes were cast on the ground, without looking in any other direction.

When the Captain came before him, he said, through the interpreter, that he was a Captain sent by the Governor to express the great desire he had to see him, and that if he would come the Governor would greatly rejoice; and the Captain added other arguments. He gave no answer, nor did he even raise his eyes to look at the Captain. But a Chief replied to what the Captain had said. At this juncture the other Captain arrived where the first Captain had left his men, and, asking what had become of him, they answered that he had gone to speak with the Cacique.

[8] Don Alonzo Enriquez says that Soto forced his horse's head over the head of Atahuallpa, when he was sitting in state, so that the breath from the horse's nostrils moved the fringe on the Ynca's forehead. Soto was astonished that, though he had never seen a horse before, he was not in the least terrified, nor did he even raise his head (p. 92).

[9] The *llautu* or Ynca ensign of sovereignty. It is thus described by Pedro Pizarro :—" Plaits made of coloured wool, the thickness of a middle finger. They are worn in the manner of a crown, not with points, but round, and the width of a man's hand. Over the forehead was a fringe also the width of a man's hand, or a little more, of very fine wool cut in very equal lengths, and enlaced half way down with very small threads of gold, very skilfully. This wool was spun, with the lower ends untwisted, being those which fell over the forehead. The fringe reached to the eyebrows, and covered all the forehead."

Leaving his people, he crossed the river, and, on approaching near to where Atabaliba was seated, the other Captain said : " This is a brother of the Governor, who comes to see you." Then Atabaliba raised his eyes and said : " Malça-bilica,[1] a Captain that I have on the river of Turicara,[2] sent to say that you ill-treat the Caciques and put them in chains, and he sent me a collar of iron, and they say that he killed three Christians and a horse. But I intend to go to-morrow to see the Governor, and to be a friend of the Christians, because they are good." Hernando Pizarro answered : " Malçabilica is a scoundrel, and neither he nor all the Indians of that river together could kill a single Christian. How could they kill either a Christian or a horse, seeing that they are mere chickens ? The Governor and the Christians do not ill-treat the Caciques unless they are hostile, and those who are friendly are treated very well. Those who make war are attacked until they are destroyed. When you see what the Christians do, when they help you in your wars against your enemies, you will know that Malçabilica told lies to you." Atabaliba said : " A Cacique refuses to obey me. My troops will go with yours, and you will make war upon him ?" Hernando Pizarro replied, " On account of one Cacique, it is not necessary that you should send any of your Indians, though you have so large a force. Ten Christians on horseback will suffice to destroy him."

Atabaliba laughed, and said that they should drink. The Captains excused themselves from drinking the Indian liquor by saying that they were fasting ; but they were importuned by him, and accepted. Presently women came with vases of gold containing chicha of maize. When Ata-

---

[1] A chief in the valley of Turicara or Chira.

[2] Or Chira, the river on the banks of which San Miguel was originally built. Gomara says that this chief, whom he calls Maycabelica, was Chief of Poechos, on the river Chira. *Hist. de las Indias*, cap. cxiii. Hernando Pizarro speaks of him as a Chief of San Miguel.

E

baliba saw them he raised his eyes to them, and without
saying a word they went back quickly, and returned with
other larger vases of gold, and from these he gave them to
drink.[3] Afterwards they took their leave, expecting Atabaliba to come and see the Governor on the following
morning. His camp was formed on the skirts of a small
hill, the tents, which were of cotton, extending for a league,
with that of Atabaliba in the centre. All the men were on
foot outside the tents, with their arms, consisting of long
lances like pikes, stuck into the ground. There seemed to
be upwards of thirty thousand men in the camp.

When the Governor heard what had taken place, he
ordered that a good watch should be kept that night in
camp, and he commanded his Captain-General to set the
guards, and to see that the rounds were gone throughout
the night, which was accordingly done. On the Saturday
morning a messenger from Atabaliba to the Governor arrived and said : " My lord has sent me to tell you that he
wishes to come and see you, and to bring his men armed ;
for the men whom you sent yesterday were armed ; and he
desires you to send a Christian with whom he may come."
The Governor answered : " Tell your lord to come when and
how he pleases, and that, in what way soever he may come,
I will receive him as a friend and brother. I do not send
him a Christian, because it is not our custom so to send
from one lord to another."[4] The messenger set out with
this answer, and, as soon as he reached the camp, the
sentries saw that the Indians were in motion. In a short
time another messenger arrived, and said to the Governor :

---

[3] Titu Atauchi, the brother of Atahuallpa, told Felipillo, the interpreter, to ask the Spaniards to drink. Both he, and another brother
named Chuqui-huaman, pledged the Spaniards in bumpers of chicha.
The girls then brought many kinds of fresh and dried fruits, and one of
them, named Pillac Sisa Ñusta, addressed the guests, and begged them
to partake for the sake of friendship (*Garcilasso de la Vega*).

[4] Hernando Pizarro says he did send the Christian.

"Atabaliba sends me to say that he has no wish to bring his troops armed, and, though they will come with him, many will come without arms, because he wishes to bring them with him and to lodge them in the town : and they are to prepare a lodging in the *plaza,* where he will rest, which is the house known as the house of the serpent, because there is a serpent of stone within it." The Governor replied : " So let it be, and I pray that he may come quickly, for I desire to see him."

Very soon they saw the plain full of men, halting at intervals, to wait for those who were filing out of the camp. The march of the troops along the road continued until the afternoon ; and they came in separate detachments. Having passed all the narrow places on the road, they reached the ground close to the camp of the Christians, and still troops kept issuing from the camp of the Indians. Presently the Governor ordered all the Spaniards to arm themselves secretly in their lodgings, and to keep the horses saddled and bridled, and under the orders of three captains,[5] but none were to show themselves in the open space. The Captain of the artillery was ordered to have his guns pointed towards the enemy on the plain, and, when the time came, to fire. Men were stationed in the streets leading to the open space, and, taking twenty men with him, the Governor went to his lodging. These had the duty entrusted to them of seizing the person of Atabaliba, if he should come cautiously with so large a force as was coming ; but the Governor ordered that he should be taken alive. All the troops had orders not to leave their quarters, even if the enemy should enter the open space, until they should hear the guns fired off. The sentries were to be on the alert, and, if they saw that the enemy intended treachery, they

[5] The three squadrons of horse, each numbering twenty, were commanded by Hernando, Gonzalo, and Juan Pizarro, with the Captains Hernando de Soto and Sebastian de Benalcazar (*Zarate,* lib. ii, cap. v).

were to give the signal; and all were to sally out of the
lodgings, the cavalry mounted, when they heard the cry of
Santiago.

Having made these arrangements, the Governor waited
for the appearance of Atabaliba; but no Christian was in
sight except the sentry, who gave notice of what was
passing in the army of the Indians. The Governor and
Captain-General visited the quarters of the Spaniards, seeing
that they were ready to sally forth when it was necessary,
saying to them all that they must be of good courage, and
make fortresses of their hearts, for that they had no others,
and no hope but in God, who would help those who worked
in his service, even in their greatest need. He told them that
though, for every Christian, there were five hundred Indians,
yet they must have that reliance which good men find on
such occasions, and they must trust that God would fight on
their side. He told them that, at the moment of attacking,
they must come out with desperate fury and break through
the enemy, taking care that the horses do not hinder each
other. These and similar exhortations were made by the
Governor and Captain-General to the Christians, to raise
their spirits, and they were more ready to come forth than to
remain in their lodgings. Each man was ready to encounter
a hundred, and they felt very little fear at seeing so great a
multitude.

When the Governor saw that it was near sunset, and that
Atabaliba did not move from the place to which he had re-
paired, although troops still kept issuing out of his camp,
he sent a Spaniard to ask him to come into the square to
see him before it was dark. As soon as the messenger came
before Atabaliba, he made an obeisance to him, and made
signs that he should come to where the Governor waited.
Presently he and his troops began to move, and the Spaniard
returned and reported that they were coming, and that the
men in front carried arms concealed under their clothes,

which were strong tunics of cotton, beneath which were
stones and bags and slings ; all which made it appear that
they had a treacherous design. Soon the van of the enemy
began to enter the open space. First came a squadron of
Indians dressed in a livery of different colours, like a chess
board.[6] They advanced, removing the straws from the
ground, and sweeping the road. Next came three squadrons
in different dresses, dancing and singing. Then came a
number of men with armour, large metal plates, and crowns
of gold and silver. Among them was Atabaliba[7] in a litter
lined with plumes of macaws' feathers, of many colours, and
adorned with plates of gold and silver. Many Indians carried it on their shoulders on high.[8] Next came two other
litters and two hammocks, in which were some principal
chiefs ; and lastly, several squadrons of Indians with crowns
of gold and silver.

As soon as the first entered the open space they moved
aside and gave space to the others. On reaching the centre
of the open space, Atabaliba remained in his litter on high,
and the others with him, while his troops did not cease to
enter.[9] A captain then came to the front and, ascending
the fortress near the open space, where the artillery was
posted, raised his lance twice, as for a signal.[1] Seeing this,

---

[6] First came three hundred youths with bows and arrows, singing,
and cleaning the road with their hands. Then came a thousand men
with pikes, having no iron tips, but with the points hardened in the fire.
They wore a livery of white and red squares, like a chess board. A
third squadron then entered, with hammers of copper and silver. (Relacion del Primer Descubrimiento MS.)

[7] He wore a collar of large emeralds. (Relacion, etc.)

[8] It was borne by eighty chiefs, all dressed in a very rich blue livery.
(Relacion, etc.)

[9] Seeing no Spaniards, he said to his captains :—" Where are these
Christians, that they do not appear?" They answered :—" Lord ! the
Christians are hidden, for they are afraid." (Pedro Pizarro).

[1] Hernando Pizarro does not appear to have thought that any signal
was intended. He says that a few Indians went into the fort, and

the Governor asked the Father Friar Vicente if he wished
to go and speak to Atabaliba, with an interpreter? He
replied that he did wish it, and he advanced, with a cross in
one hand and the Bible in the other,[2] and going amongst
the troops up to the place where Atabaliba was, thus addressed him : " I am a Priest of God, and I teach Christians
the things of God, and in like manner I come to teach you.
What I teach is that which God says to us in this Book.
Therefore, on the part of God and of the Christians, I beseech
you to be their friend, for such is God's will, and it will be
for your good. Go and speak to the Governor, who waits
for you."

Atabaliba asked for the Book, that he might look at it,
and the Priest gave it to him closed. Atabaliba did not
know how to open it, and the Priest was extending his arm
to do so, when Atabaliba, in great anger, gave him a blow
on the arm, not wishing that it should be opened. Then he
opened it himself, and, without any astonishment at the
letters and paper, as had been shown by other Indians, he
threw it away from him five or six paces, and, to the words
which the monk had spoken to him through the interpreter,
he answered with much scorn, saying: " I know well how you
have behaved on the road, how you have treated my Chiefs,
and taken the cloth from my storehouses." The Monk replied : " The Christians have not done this, but some
Indians took the cloth without the knowledge of the
Governor, and he ordered it to be restored." Atabaliba
said : " I will not leave this place until they bring it all to
me." The Monk returned with this reply to the Governor.
Atabaliba stood up on the top of the litter, addressing his

planted a lance with a banner at the end, by way of taking possession.
It was probably no more than a sign of the royal presence; like hoisting
the standard at Windsor.

    [2] He was accompanied by Hernando de Aldana, and an interpreter
named Martinillo.

troops and ordering them to be prepared. The Monk told
the Governor what had passed between him and Atabaliba,
and that he had thrown the Scriptures to the ground.[3]
Then the Governor put on a jacket of cotton, took his sword
and dagger, and, with the Spaniards who were with him,
entered amongst the Indians most valiantly; and, with only
four men who were able to follow him, he came to the litter
where Atabaliba was, and fearlessly seized him by the arm,
crying out *Santiago*. Then the guns were fired off, the
trumpets were sounded, and the troops, both horse and foot,
sallied forth.[4] On seeing the horses charge, many of the
Indians who were in the open space fled, and such was the
force with which they ran that they broke down part of the
wall surrounding it, and many fell over each other. The
horsemen rode them down, killing and wounding, and following in pursuit. The infantry made so good an assault
upon those that remained that in a short time most of them
were put to the sword. The Governor still held Atabaliba
by the arm, not being able to pull him out of the litter because he was raised so high. Then the Spaniards made
such a slaughter amongst those who carried the litter that
they fell to the ground, and, if the Governor had not pro-
tected Atabaliba, that proud man would there have paid for
all the cruelties he had committed. The Governor, in protecting Atabaliba, received a slight wound in the hand.
During the whole time no Indian raised his arms against a

---

[3] The Monk said:—"See you not what is happening? Why are you
treating with this proud dog, when the plain is covered with Indians.
Fall upon him. I absolve you." (*Relacion*, etc.)

Don Alonzo Enriquez says:—"Then the rascally friar, who was certainly a peace-breaker, began to call with a loud voice, saying, ' Christians, I call upon you to avenge this insult to the faith of Jesus Christ'."
(P. 93).

[4] "At that sound we all came out as one man, for these houses, facing
the *plaza*, had many doors, so it seemed as if they had been built for this
business". (*Relacion*, etc.)

Spaniard. So great was the terror of the Indians at seeing the Governor force his way through them, at hearing the fire of the artillery, and beholding the charging of the horses, a thing never before heard of, that they thought more of flying to save their lives than of fighting. All those who bore the litter of Atabaliba appeared to be principal chiefs. They were all killed, as well as those who were carried in the other litters and hammocks. One of them was the page of Atabaliba, and a great lord, and the others were lords of many vassals, and his Councillors. The chief of Caxamalca was also killed, and others; but, the number being very great, no account was taken of them, for all who came in attendance on Atabaliba were great lords. The Governor went to his lodging, with his prisoner Atabaliba, despoiled of his robes, which the Spaniards had torn off in pulling him out of the litter. It was a very wonderful thing to see so great a lord taken prisoner in so short a time, who came in such power. The Governor presently ordered native clothes to be brought, and when Atabaliba was dressed, he made him sit near him, and soothed his rage and agitation at finding himself so quickly fallen from his high estate. Among many other things, the Governor said to him : "Do not take it as an insult that you have been defeated and taken prisoner, for with the Christians who come with me, though so few in number, I have conquered greater kingdoms than yours, and have defeated other more powerful lords than you, imposing upon them the dominion of the Emperor, whose vassal I am, and who is King of Spain and of the universal world. We come to conquer this land by his command, that all may come to a knowledge of God, and of His Holy Catholic Faith ; and by reason of our good object, God, the Creator of heaven and earth and of all things in them, permits this, in order that you may know him, and come out from the bestial and diabolical life you lead. It is for this reason that we, being so few in number, subjugate that vast host. When you have seen the errors in which you live, you will understand the good we have done you by coming to your land by order of his Majesty. You should consider it to be your good fortune that you have not been defeated by a cruel people, such as you are yourselves, who grant life to none. We treat our prisoners and conquered enemies with kindness, and only make war on those who attack us, and, being able to destroy them, we refrain from doing so, but rather pardon them. When I had a Chief, the lord of an island, my prisoner, I set him free that henceforth he might be loyal; and I did the same with the Chiefs who were lords of Tumbez and Chilimasa, and others who, being in my power, and deserving death, I pardoned. If you were seized, and your people attacked and killed, it was because you came against us with so great an army, having sent to say that you would come peacefully, and because you threw the Book to the ground in which is written the words of God. Therefore our Lord permitted that your pride should be brought low, and that no Indian should be able to offend a Christian."

After the Governor had delivered this discourse, Atabaliba thus replied: "I was deceived by my Captains, who told me to think lightly of the Spaniards. I desired to come peacefully, but they prevented me, but all those who thus advised me are now dead. I have now seen the goodness and daring of the Spaniards, and that Malçabilica lied in all the news he sent me touching the Christians."

As it was now night, and the Governor saw that those who had gone in pursuit of the Indians were not returned, he ordered the guns to be fired and the trumpets to be sounded to recall them. Soon afterwards they returned to the camp with a great crowd of people whom they had taken alive, numbering more than three thousand. The Governor asked whether they were all well. His Captain-General, who went with them, answered that only one horse had a slight

wound. The Governor, with great joy, said: "I give
thanks to God our Lord, and we all, gentlemen, ought to
give thanks for the great miracle we have wrought this day.
In truth we ought to believe that, without His special help,
we could not have entered this land, how much less have
conquered so great a host. God, in His mercy, sees fit to
grant these favours, and we should give Him thanks for
His great works, that we may conquer this kingdom. But,
gentlemen, you must be fatigued, and I, therefore, desire
you to retire to rest. Although we have the victory, we
must still be watchful. The enemy is defeated, but he is
cunning and experienced in war. This lord too, as we
know, is feared and obeyed, and they will try every artifice
to rescue him. This night, and every night, there must be
good watch kept, and the rounds must be gone regularly,
that we may be prepared for any event."

So they went to supper, and the Governor caused Atabaliba to sit at the table, treating him well, and they served
him in the same way as the Governor. Orders were then
given that he was to have such of his imprisoned women as
he desired for his service, to wait on him, and a good bed
was prepared for him in the same chamber where the
Governor slept. He was allowed to remain unconfined, and
without being kept in prison, but was watched by guards.[5]
The battle lasted only about half an hour, for the sun had
already set when it commenced. If the night had not come
on, few out of the thirty thousand men that came would
have been left. It is the opinion of some, who have seen
armies in the field, that there were more than forty thousand
men. In the square and on the plain there were two thousand killed, besides wounded. A wonderful thing was ob-

---

[5] Don Alonzo Enriquez tells us that, in twenty days, Atahuallpa had
learnt to speak Spanish, and to play at chess and cards. He also asked
men to write down words that he knew, and got others to read them ;
and thus he acquired a knowledge of the art of writing. (Pp. 92, 93).

served in this battle.   It was that the horses which, the day
before, could scarcely move for the cold, were able to charge
with such fury that they seemed as if nothing had ever ailed
them.   The Captain-General set the watches and rounds for
that night, stationing them at convenient points.   Next
morning the Governor sent a Captain, with thirty horse, to
scour the plain, and he ordered them to break the arms of
the Indians.   The troops in the camp made the imprisoned
Indians remove the dead bodies from the open space.   The
Captain, with his horsemen, collected all that was on the
plain and in the tents of Atabaliba, and returned to the
camp before noon with a troop of men, women, sheep, gold,
silver, and cloth.   Among these spoils there were eighty
thousand *pesos*, seven thousand marcs of silver, and fourteen
emeralds.   The gold and silver were in immense pieces,
great and small plates and jars, pots, cups, and other shapes.
Atabaliba said that all this was the furniture of his service,
and that the Indians who fled had taken a great deal more
away with them.   The Governor ordered all the sheep to be
set free, because there was a great multitude, and they en-
cumbered the camp.   The Christians could kill daily as
many as they required.   The Indians, who had been captured the night before, were ordered to be collected in the
open space, that the Christians might take those they required for their service.   All the rest were ordered to be set
free, and to return to their homes, for they belonged to
different provinces, and Atabaliba had brought them away
to assist in his wars, and for the service of his army.

    Some were of opinion that all the Indian soldiers should
be killed, or, at least, that their hands should be cut off.
The Governor would not consent, saying that it would not
be well to commit so great a cruelty, for, although the power
of Atabaliba was great, and he was able to collect a vast multitude of people, yet the power of our Lord God is, beyond all
comparison, greater ; and He grants aid to His own through

His infinite goodness.   He added that they should be certain that He who had delivered them from the danger of the
previous day would also protect them hereafter, seeing that
the intentions of the Christians were good in bringing these
infidel barbarians to the service of God and to a knowledge
of our Holy Catholic Faith.   They should not desire to be
like those Indians, in their cruelties and sacrifices, which
they perpetrate on those they capture in war.   Those who
died in the battle were more than enough; and the prisoners,
who had been brought in like sheep into a fold, should not
be killed nor injured.   They were, therefore, set free.

In this town of Caxamalca, certain houses were found full
of cloth, packed in bales which reached to the roof.   They
say that it was a depôt to supply the army.   The Christians
took what they required, and yet the house remained so full
that what was taken seemed hardly to be missed.   The cloth
was the best that had been seen in the Indies.   The greater
part of it is of very fine wool, and the rest of cotton of rich
colours, beautifully variegated.   The arms they found, with
which they made war, and their manner of fighting were as
follows.   In the van of their armies came the sling-men, who
hurled pebbles from slings.   These sling-men carry shields,
which they make from narrow boards very small.   They also
wear jackets of quilted cotton.   Next came men armed with
sticks having large knobs at one end, and axes.   The sticks
are a *braça* and a half in length, and the thickness of a lance.
The knob at the end is of metal, with five or six sharp points,
each point being as thick as a man's thumb.   They use
them with both hands.   The axes were the same size or
larger.   The metal blade was a *palmo* in width, like a
halberd.   Some of the axes and clubs, used by the chiefs,
were of gold and silver.   Behind these came men armed
with hurling lances, like darts.   In the rear were pikemen
with lances thirty *palmos* in length.   These men had sleeves
with many folds of cotton, over which they worked the lances.

They are all divided into squadrons, with their banners and captains who command them, with as much order as Turks. Some of them wear great head pieces of wood, with many folds of cotton, reaching to the eyes, which could not be stronger if they were of iron. The men who composed the army of Atabaliba were all very dexterous and experienced soldiers, who had served in it from boys. They were young and stout, and only a thousand of them sufficed to assault a town of that land, though it were garrisoned with twenty thousand men.

The lodging of Atabaliba, which he had in the centre of his camp, was the best that had been seen in the Indies, though it was small. It consisted of four rooms, with a court in the centre, having a pond supplied with water by a tube, and this water was so warm that one could not bear to put a hand into it.[6] This water rises out of an adjacent mountain. Another tube brought cold water, and the two united in one tube on the road, and flowed, mixed together, by a single tube, into the pond. When they wish to allow one sort to flow alone, they remove the tube of the other. The pond is large and paved with stone. Outside the house, in a part of the yard, there is another pond, not so well made. They both have their flights of stone steps, by which to go down and bathe. The room in which Atabaliba stayed during the day was a corridor looking into an orchard, and near it there is a chamber where he slept, with a window looking towards the court and the pond. The corridor also opens on the court. The walls were plastered with a red bitumen, better than ochre, which shined much, and the wood, which formed the eaves of the house, was of the same colour. Another room is composed of four vaults, like bells, united into one. This is plastered with lime, as

[6] Humboldt mentions the columns of smoke, seen at a distance, rising from the warm springs of Pultamarca, which are called the " Baths of the Ynca". The temperature of these sulphur springs was found to be 156 degs. 2 min. Fahr.

white as snow. The other two are offices. A river flows in front of this palace.[7]

Now that an account has been given of the victory of the Christians and the capture of Atabaliba, and of the ordering of his camp and army, I will proceed to say something concerning the father of this Atabaliba, and how he was made lord, besides other things relating to his grandeur, as they were described to the Governor by Atabaliba himself. The father of this Atabaliba was called the Cuzco,[8] and he ruled over all that land, for an extent of more than three hundred leagues, in which the people obeyed him and paid him tribute. He was a native of a province called Quito ;[9] but, as he found the land, where he was encamped, to be pleasant, fertile, and rich, he settled there, and gave the name to a great city where he lived, which was called the city of the Cuzco.[1] He was so feared and obeyed that they almost looked upon him as their god, and his image was set up in many towns. He had a hundred sons and daughters, most of them being still alive. It is eight years since he died, and he left as his heir a son of the same name as his own. He was a son of his legitimate wife. They call the principal wife, who is most loved by the husband, legitimate.[2] This son was older than Atabaliba. The old Cuzco separated the province of Quito from the rest of the kingdom, and left it to Atabaliba. The body of the Cuzco is in the province of Quito, where he died, and his head was conveyed to the city of Cuzco, where they hold it in great veneration, adorning it with gold and silver.[3]

[7] Some slight remains of this palace were visible in Humboldt's time.

[8] The Ynca Huayna Ccapac.

[9] This is a mistake. It was Atahuallpa, not his father, who was a native of Quito.

[1] Xeres here makes a most extraordinary blunder, confusing the name of the city with that of the Ynca.

[2] Another blunder. The legitimate wife was the sister, or at least the first cousin of the Ynca, of pure Ynca descent on both sides.

[3] Another blunder. The body and head of Huayna Ccapac were con-

The house in which it is kept is all plated with gold and
silver, the one metal interwoven with the other. In this
city there are twenty other houses with walls covered with
thin gold leaf, both within and without. This city contains
very rich edifices. In it the Cuzco had his treasury, consisting of three chambers full of pieces of gold, five full of
silver, and one hundred thousand lumps of gold taken from
the mines, each lump weighing fifty *castellanos*. This has
been tribute from the lands that have been subjugated.
Beyond this city there is another called Collao, where there
is a river containing much gold.[4] Ten days' journey from
this province of Caxamalca, in another province called
Guaneso,[5] there is another river as rich as the one before
mentioned. In all these provinces there are many mines of
gold and silver. They get the silver out of the mountains
with little trouble, one Indian getting five or six *marcs* in a
single day. They find it with lead, tin, and sulphur, and
afterwards they purify it. They get it out by burning the
hill, and, as the sulphur stone burns, the silver falls in
lumps. The distance from here to the city of Cuzco is
forty days' journey of a laden Indian, and the country is
well peopled. Chincha is a populous district, half-way.[6]
Throughout the land there are many flocks of sheep, and
many are wild because they cannot maintain as many as
they breed. Among the Spaniards who accompany the
Governor they kill one hundred and fifty every day, and yet

veyed together to Cuzco; though he died at Tumi-pampa. The body
was discovered by the Spaniards and taken to Lima. See the account
in *Garcilasso*, i, p. 273.

[4] The Collao is the name of the region drained by streams flowing into
lake Titicaca. The river, containing gold, is of course in Caravaya, beyond the eastern Cordillera.

[5] Probably Huanuco, and the river Huallaga.

[6] They seem often to have heard of Chincha. It is a valley on the
coast. But Xeres confuses it with one of the four great divisions of the
Ynca empire, called Chincha-suyu, which includes Cassamarca.

there would be no scarcity if they remained in this valley throughout the year. The Indians usually eat them in all parts of the land.

Atabaliba also said that after the death of his father he and his brother were at peace for seven years, each one in the land which their father had left them. But a little more than a year ago his brother rose against him with the design of depriving him of his government. Afterwards Atabaliba sent to beg him not to make war, but to be content with what his father had left him, but the Cuzco was not satisfied with this. Then Atabaliba departed from his land, which is called Quito, with all the soldiers he could collect, and came to Tomepomba,[7] where he fought a battle with his brother. In this encounter Atabaliba and his troops killed more than a thousand of the men of Cuzco, and made him take to flight. He also slew all the people in Tomepomba because they attempted to defend the place; and he intended to destroy all the villages in the district, but he refrained because he wished to pursue his brother. The Cuzco fled to his own land, and Atabaliba advanced, conquering the provinces, while all the cities, remembering the fate of Tomepomba, voluntarily submitted. It is six months since Atabaliba sent two of his attendants, very valiant men, the one called Quisquis and the other Chaliachin,[8] who advanced with forty thousand men against the city of his brother, gaining all the land up to that on which the city stands, which they captured. They then killed many people, took the brother prisoner, and seized all the treasure of the father. When this news came to Atabaliba, he ordered his brother to be brought to him as a prisoner; and there is news that they will soon arrive with him, and with much treasure. The captains remained in the city they had conquered to guard it and the treasure it contains. They kept ten thousand men as a garrison, out of forty thousand they

---

[7] Tumi-pampa.   [8] Chalcuchima.

took with them, and the other thirty thousand went to rest at their homes with the spoils they had secured. Atabaliba conquered all that his brother once possessed.

Atabaliba and his Captains General who were carried in litters, have killed many people since the war began; and Atabaliba has perpetrated many cruelties on his enemies. He has with him all the chiefs of the villages he has conquered, and has put his own governors in all the villages, otherwise he could not keep the country so quiet, and thus he has been feared and obeyed, and his soldiers have been well served by the people, who have also been treated well. Atabaliba intended, if his imprisonment had not come upon him, to go and rest in his own land, and, on his way, to complete the destruction of all the villages in the district of Tomepomba[9] which had attempted to defend themselves; peopling them with new families. For this purpose his captains had sent four thousand married men of the people of Cuzco to settle in Tomepomba. Atabaliba also said that he would deliver his brother, whom his captains were bringing a prisoner to this city, into the hands of the Governor, to do with him as he pleased. Atabaliba feared that the Spaniards would kill him, so he told the Governor, that he would give his captors a great quantity of gold and silver. The Governor asked him : " How much can you give, and in what time ?" Atabaliba said : " I will give gold enough to fill a room twenty-two feet long and seventeen wide, up to a white line which is half way up the wall." The height would be that of a man's stature and a half. He said that, up to that mark, he would fill the room with different kinds of golden vessels, such as jars, pots, vases, besides lumps and other pieces. As for silver, he said he would fill the whole chamber with it twice over. He undertook to do this in two months. The Governor told him to send off messengers with this object, and that, when it was accomplished, he need

9 Tumi-pampa.

F

have no fear. Then Atabaliba sent messages to his captains,
who were in the city of Cuzco, ordering them to send two
thousand Indians laden with gold and silver, without counting that which was coming with his brother, whom they
were bringing as a prisoner. The Governor asked him :
" How long will your messengers take to go to the city of
Cuzco ?" Atabaliba said : "When they are sent, with speed,
to carry some tidings, they run by post from village to
village, and go over the distance in five days. But if the
man who starts with the message goes the whole way,
though he be an agile man, he will take fifteen days." The
Governor also asked him : " Why did you order some
Indians to be killed, whom the Christians found dead in
your camp when they examined it ?" Atabaliba answered :
" On the day that the Governor sent his brother, Hernando
Pizarro, to the camp to speak with me, one of the Christians
charged with his horse, and these men that are dead ran
back. That is the reason that I ordered them to be killed."

Atabaliba was a man of thirty years of age, good looking,
somewhat stout, with a fine face, handsome and fierce, the
eyes bloodshot.[1] He spoke with much dignity, like a great
lord. He talked with good arguments, and reasoned well,
and when the Spaniards understood what he said, they knew
him to be a wise man. He was cheerful ; but, when he
spoke to his subjects, he was very haughty, and showed no
sign of pleasure. Among other things, Atabaliba said to
the Governor : " Ten days' journey from Caxamalca, on the
road to Cuzco, there is, in a village, a mosque,[2] which all the
inhabitants of that land look upon as their common temple.
In it they all offer up gold and silver, and my father
held it in great veneration, as well as myself. This mosque
contains great riches, for, though there is a mosque in each

---

[1] He wore his mantle over his head, covering one ear, which had been
broken through in his war with Huascar (*Pedro Pizarro*).

[2] Pachacamac, on the coast.

village where they have their special idols which they worship, in this mosque there is a general idol common to all, and there is a famous sage in charge of that mosque, whom the Indians believe to have a knowledge of future events, because he speaks to that idol." Having heard these words (though he had already heard of this mosque), the Governor gave Atabaliba to understand: " All those idols are vanity, and he who speaks from them is the Devil, who deceives men and brings them to perdition, a fate which has befallen all those who have lived in that belief, and so died. But God is one sole Creator of heaven and earth, and of all things visible and invisible, and in this the Christians believe. Him only ought we to hold as God, and we are bound to do what he commands, and to receive the waters of baptism. Those who thus act will be received into His kingdom, and the others will go to the punishment of hell, where those are burning for ever who were without this knowledge, and who have served the Devil, making sacrifices and offerings, and building mosques to him. All these things from henceforth must cease, because for this the Emperor, who is king and lord of the Christians, has sent us. It was because your people had lived as they have lived without a knowledge of God that he allowed so great an army of them to be defeated and taken prisoners by a few Christians. How little help your God has given you! By this you may know that he is the Devil who deceives you." Atabaliba said: " Until now I have never seen Christians, nor have my ancestors known anything of these things; and I have lived as they lived." He added: " I am amazed at what you have said; and I well know that the idol is not the true God, seeing that he gave me so little help."

As soon as the Governor and the Spaniards were rested from the fatigues of the journey and of the battle, he sent news to the citizens of San Miguel of what had happened, and inquiries as to their well-being, and whether any ships had arrived. He then ordered a church to be prepared in the square of Caxamalca, in which to celebrate the Holy Sacrament of the Mass. He also ordered the wall surrounding the square to be pulled down, because it was too low, and a higher wall to be built. In four days a wall was built, two men's lengths in height, and five hundred and fifty paces long. He also caused other precautions to be taken for the safety of the camp. Each day it was reported to him whether there was any concourse of people, and what things happened in the surrounding country.

When the chiefs of this province heard of the arrival of the Governor, and of the imprisonment of Atabaliba, many of them came peacefully to see the Governor. Some of these chiefs were lords of thirty thousand Indians, all subject to Atabaliba. When they came before him, they made great obeisances, kissing his feet and hands. He received them without looking at them. It was a strange thing this gravity of Atabaliba, and the reverence with which they all treated him. Every day they brought him many presents from all parts of the land. Thus, prisoner as he was, he had the state of a lord, and was very cheerful. It is true that the Governor treated him very well; though sometimes he told him that Indians had informed the Spaniards of an assemblage of his troops in Guamachuco,[3] and other parts. Atabaliba replied that throughout that land there was no one who would move without his permission; if, therefore, his warriors should come, the Governor might take it for certain that he had ordered them to come, and that then he could do with him as he pleased, for was he not his prisoner. The Indians said many things which were not true, although they gave rise to some excitement

[3] Huamachuco, which Cieza de Leon states to be eleven leagues south of Cassa-marca. See my translations of *Cieza de Leon*, p. 287, and of *Garcilasso de la Vega*, ii, p. 137.

among the Spaniards. Among many messengers who came to Atabaliba, there came one from those who were bringing his brother a prisoner, to report that, as soon as they had heard of his imprisonment, they had killed the Cuzco.[4] When the Governor knew this, he showed much displeasure. Then Atabaliba said that the news was false, that the Cuzco had not been killed, and that he would presently arrive, and that, if not, the Governor might order him to be killed. Afterwards Atabaliba declared that his captains had killed the Cuzco without his knowledge. The Governor obtained the news from the messengers, and knew that he had been killed.

After some days some of the people of Atabaliba arrived. There was a brother of his, who came from Cuzco, and sisters and wives. The brother brought many vases, jars, and pots of gold, and much silver, and he said that more was on the road; but that, as the journey is so long, the Indians who bring the treasure become tired, and cannot all come so quickly, so that every day more gold and silver will arrive of that which now remains behind. Thus on some days twenty thousand, on others thirty thousand, on others fifty thousand or sixty thousand *pesos* of gold arrived, in vases, great pots weighing two or three *arrobas*, and other vessels. The Governor ordered it all to be put in the house where Atabaliba had his guards, until he had accomplished what he had promised. Twenty days of the month of December had passed, when messengers arrived from San Miguel with a letter which informed the Governor that six ships had arrived at the port of Cancebi, near Quaque. They brought one hundred and fifty Spaniards and eighty-four horses. The three larger ships came from Panama, and on board them were the Captain Diego de Almagro and one hundred and twenty men. The other three caravels

[4] Huascar is said to have been drowned in the river of Anta-marca. See *Herrera*, Dec. v, lib. ii, cap. 2.

were from Nicarague with thirty men, who came to this government with the desire to serve in it. From Cancebi, after they had landed the troops and horses, a vessel was sent to find out where the Governor was, and she arrived at Tumbez ; but the chief of that province would give no information, and did not show the letter which the Governor left to be given to the ships that might arrive. So the ships returned without obtaining news of the Governor. Another vessel, which followed the first along the coast, arrived at the port of San Miguel, where the master landed and went to the town. There was great rejoicing at his arrival, and he returned with the letters which the Governor had sent to the citizens, announcing the victory which God had granted to him and his people, and the great riches of the land. The Governor, and all who were with him, were much pleased at the arrival of these ships. He sent messengers with letters to the Captain Diego de Almagro and some persons who were with him, telling them how greatly he rejoiced at their arrival ; and that, as soon as they came to San Miguel (that they might avoid a stress of provisions), they should depart presently, and march to the neighbouring districts, on the road to Caxamalca, where there is great abundance. He added that he would arrange about sending down gold to pay the freight of the ships that they might return.

Every day chiefs came to the Governor. Among others, two chiefs came who were called chiefs of the thieves, because their people attacked all who passed through their land, which is on the road to Cuzco. After Atabaliba had been in prison for sixty days, the chief of the village in which the mosque stands,[5] and the guardian of the mosque arrived before the Governor, and he asked Atabaliba who they were. Atabaliba said that one was the chief of the village of the mosque, and that the other was the keeper of

<hr>

[5] Pachacamac.

it, and that he rejoiced at his arrival, because he could now pay him out for the lies he had told. Atabaliba then begged the Governor to put the keeper in chains because it was he that advised the war with the Christians, saying that the idol had foretold that all would be killed. He had also told his father, the Cuzco, when he was on the point of death, that he would not die of that disease. The Governor ordered the chain to be brought, and Atabaliba put it on, saying that it should not be taken off until the keeper had caused all the gold of the mosque to be brought. Atabaliba told the keeper that he wished the riches of the mosque to be given to the Christians because the idol was a liar; and he added: "I wish to see whether this that you call your God will free you from your chains." The Governor and the chief, who came with the keeper, sent their messengers to bring the gold of the mosque and that belonging to the chief, and it was said that they could return in fifty days. The Governor had information that there were assemblies of men in the land, and that there were soldiers at Guamachuco. So he sent Hernando Pizarro, with twenty horse and some foot, to Guamachuco, which is three days' journey from Caxamalca, to learn what was going on, and to bring the gold and silver that was in Guamachuco. The Captain Hernando Pizarro set out from Caxamalca on the eve of the Epiphany, in the year 1533. Fifteen days afterwards some Christians arrived at Caxamalca with a great quantity of gold and silver. There were more than three hundred loads of gold and silver in jars and great vases and in divers other shapes. The Governor ordered it all to be placed with the first that had been brought, where Atabaliba had his guards stationed. He kept it there, saying that he wished to keep an account, as he had to accomplish what he had promised; that when it had all come, he might deliver up the whole. In order that the account might be correct, the Governor also guarded the treasure-house night and day; and when

it was deposited in the house each piece was counted, that
there might be no fraud.   With this gold and silver came a
brother of Atabaliba, who said that there was still a great
quantity on the road at Xauxa, in charge of one of the
Captains of Atabaliba, named Chilicuchima.[6]   Hernando
Pizarro wrote to the Governor that he had informed himself
touching what was going on in the land, and that there was
no news of any assemblages, nor of anything else, except
that the gold was at Xauxa, in charge of a Captain.   He
desired to know what he should do, and whether he should
advance, adding that he would remain where he was until
he received further orders.   The Governor answered that he
was to proceed to the mosque, as he detained the keeper of
it as his prisoner, and Atabaliba had ordered its treasure to
be brought to Caxamalca.   His orders, therefore, were to
march at once and secure all the gold that could be found in
the mosque, writing a report from every village of what had
happened on the road.

Seeing the delay there was in bringing the gold, the
Governor sent three Christians to fetch the gold that was at
Xauxa, and to see the city of Cuzco.[7]   He also gave powers

<hr/>

[6] Chalcuchima.

[7] Pizarro appears first to have sent three soldiers named Pedro Moguer,
Francisco de Zarate, and Martin Bueno ; but, on their arrival at Cuzco,
they behaved with so much imprudence and insolence, as to endanger
their own lives and the success of their mission.   After their departure
Pizarro would seem to have doubted the wisdom of entrusting so delicate
a mission to common soldiers.   He, therefore, ordered two officers of
distinction, Hernando de Soto and Pedro del Barco, a native of Lobon,
to follow the three soldiers to Cuzco.   They travelled in litters, carried
on the shoulders of Indians.   On reaching Xauxa they met the unfor-
tunate Ynca Huascar, being brought as a prisoner to his brother Atahuallpa.   Huascar promised to give twice as much gold as it was possible
for his brother to find, if they would return with him and persuade
Pizarro to judge between him and his brother.   The Spaniards had no
interpreter ; but when the speech was reported to Atahuallpa, he sent
orders for Huascar to be murdered on the road.   See *G. de la Vega*,

to one of the three to take possession of the city of Cuzco
and its districts, in the name of his Majesty, in presence of
a notary who went with him.   He sent a brother of Atabaliba with them.   They had orders not to injure the
natives, nor to take their gold nor anything else against
their wills.   They were not to do more than the chief who
accompanied them wished them to do, lest they should be
killed; but they were to endeavour to get a sight of the
city of Cuzco, and to bring a report of all they saw.   These
men set out from Caxamalca on the 5th day of February in
the above-mentioned year.

The Captain Diego de Almagro arrived at Caxamalca
with some troops, and entered it on Easter eve, being the
14th of April of the said year, and was well received by the
Governor and those who were with him.   A negro, who set
out with the Cuzco party, returned on the 28th of April with
one hundred and seven loads of gold and seven of silver.   He
returned from Xauxa, where he met the Indians who were
coming with the gold.   The other Christians went on to Cuzco;
and the negro reported that the Captain Hernando Pizarro
would return very shortly, and that he had gone to Xauxa
to see Chilicuchima.   The Governor ordered this gold to be
put with the rest, and all the pieces to be counted.

Pt. II, lib. i, cap. 31 ; *Zarate*, II, cap. vi ; *Gomara*, cap. cxiv ; and *Herrera*, Dec. v, lib. i, cap. 1.

Of the two Spaniards who visited Cuzco, Hernando de Soto achieved
immortal fame as the discoverer of Florida.   The fate of Pedro del
Barco was less fortunate.   He received half the convent of the Virgins
of the Sun as his share of the spoils of Cuzco, and sold it to an apothe-
cary named Segovia, who accidentally discovered a treasure under the
pavement worth seventy-two thousand ducats.   When Gonzalo Pizarro
rose in rebellion, Pedro del Barco fled from Cuzco, but he was seized at
Lima by Gonzalo's cruel old Lieutenant Carbajal, and hanged on a tree
outside the walls of the town.   The half-caste orphan children of Barco
were adopted and treated with great kindness by Garcilasso de la Vega,
the historian's father.   One was a schoolfellow of the historian, and was
afterwards banished to Chile by the Viceroy Toledo.

On the 25th of March[8] the Captain Hernando Pizarro
entered Caxamalca with all the Christians he had taken
with him, and with the Captain Chilicuchima. The Governor gave him and his companions a very good reception.
He brought from the mosque twenty-seven loads of gold
and two thousand *marcs* of silver ; and he delivered to the
Governor the report, which was drawn up by Miguel Estete,[9]
the inspector, who accompanied him on the journey. This
report is as follows : —

THE NARRATIVE

Of the journey made by El Señor Captain Hernando Pizarro,
  by order of the Governor, his brother, from the city of
  Caxamalca to Parcama,[1] and thence to Xauxa.

On Wednesday, the day of the Epiphany (which is
vulgarly called the Festival of the three Kings), on the 5th
of January, 1533, the Captain Fernando Pizarro[2] set out
from the town of Caxamalca with twenty horse and a few
arquebusiers. On that night he rested at some huts which
were five leagues from the town. Next day he dined at
another town called Ychoca, where he was well received.
They gave him what he required for himself and his people.

---

  [8] This should be April.
  [9] Miguel Estete (or Astete) was the man who pulled the royal *llautu*
or fringe from the head of Atahuallpa, when he was dragged from his
litter. Astete kept it carefully ; and when the Viceroy, Marquis of
Cañete, raised Sayri Tupac (son of Manco and grandson of Huayna
Ccapac) to the nominal sovereignty, many years afterwards, Astete presented him with the *llautu* of Atahuallpa. Astete settled at Huamanca,
and his descendants now live at Cuzco. They were friends of the ill-
fated Tupac Amaru in 1782, and consistent opponents of Spanish tyranny.
The kindness and hospitality of the good old Señora Astete, and her intimate knowledge of Peruvian history, will long be remembered by those
who knew Cuzco twenty years ago.
  [1] Pachacamac.
  [2] He was accompanied by his brothers Juan and Gonzalo (*Herrera*).

On the same day he came to pass the night at another small village called Huancasanga, subject to the town of Guamachuco. Next morning he reached the town of Guamachuco, which is large, and is situated in a valley surrounded by mountains. It has a beautiful view and good lodgings. The Lord of the place is called Guamanchoro, by whom the Captain and his companions were well received. Here arrived a brother of Atabaliba, who was hurrying the gold up from Cuzco,[3] and the Captain learnt from him that the Captain Chilicuchima was twenty days' journey off, and that he was bringing the treasure that Atabaliba had sent for. When he found that the treasure was so far off, the Captain sent a messenger to the Governor, to ask him what should be done, adding that he would not advance until he received further orders. In this town some Indians reported that Chilicuchima was far off; and some principal men, having been bribed, stated that Chilicuchima was only seven leagues distant, in the town of Andamarca, with 20,000 men of war, and that they were coming to kill the Christians and to liberate their Lord. The chief who said this confessed that he had dined with him on the previous day. A companion of this chief, who was taken aside, made the same statement. The Captain, therefore, resolved to go in search of Chilicuchima, and, having mustered his men, he commenced the march. He passed that night at a small village, subject to Guama-

---

[3] Garcilasso says that, as Hernando Pizarro and his party were marching along a mountain side, they saw a golden line on the opposite side shining like the sun. It turned out to be a long train of Indians who had set down the golden vases they were bringing from Cuzco in rows, to rest; they were in charge of a brother of Atahuallpa, named Quilliscacha. This is the Yllescas of the Spanish writers.

The above story was told to Garcilasso by several people in Peru, and by Don Gabriel Pizarro in Spain, who had it from Don Juan Pizarro de Orellana, one of those who accompanied Hernando Pizarro to Pachacamac.

chuco, called Tambo ; and there he received the same information as had been given him before. In this village he
had a good watch kept all night, and next morning he
continued his journey with much circumspection. Before
noon he reached the town of Andamarca, but he did not
find the Captain, nor any news of him, beyond what had
first been stated by the brother of Atabaliba, that he was
in a town called Xauxa, with much gold, and that he was
on his way. In this town of Andamarca he received the
reply of the Governor, which was that Chilicuchima and
the gold were far off, that he had the bishop of the mosque
of Pachacamà in his power, and that, as to the great
wealth of gold in the mosque, the Captain should make
inquiries respecting the road, and if it seemed good to him
to go there, he might go ; as those who had gone to Cuzco
would return in the meanwhile. The Captain ascertained
the distance and the nature of the road to the mosque; and,
although his companions were badly shod,[4] and otherwise
indifferently furnished for so long a march ; he considered
that he would be doing good service in going to collect
that gold, which the Indians would not be able to bring
away ; and that it was desirable to examine that land, and
to ascertain whether it was suitable for Christian settle-
ments. Although he had information that there were many
rivers, and bridges of network, and long marches, and
difficult passes, he yet resolved to go, and he took with him
certain chiefs who knew the country.

He commenced his journey on the 14th of January, and
on the same day he crossed some difficult passes, and two
rivers, passing the night at a village called Totopamba,

---

[4] *Herrage.* The word would properly apply only to horses. The
Italian translation of Gaztelù renders it as in the text. Ternaux Compans, however, uses the word *arms* instead of *shoes.* I suspect that Xeres
really intended to say that both men and horses were badly off for shoes,
and that he used the word for horse-shoes to include all, instead of using
two words.

which is on a steep declivity.[5] The Indians received him
well and gave him good food, and all he required for the
night, and men to carry his baggage. Next day he left
this village, and reached another called Corongo, where he
passed the night. Half way there was a great pass of
snow, and all the way there were many flocks with their
shepherds, who have their houses in the mountains, as in
Spain. In this village they were given food, and all they
required, and Indians to carry the loads. This village is
subject to Guamachuco. Next day they started and came
to another small village called Piga, where they passed the
night. They found no inhabitants, as they had run away
from fear. This was a very severe march, for they had to
descend a flight of steps cut out of the stone, which was
very dangerous for the horses. Next day, at dinner time,
they reach a large village in a valley, and a very rapid river
flowed across the road. It was spanned by two bridges
close together, made of network in the following manner.
They build a foundation near the water, and raise it to a
great height ; and from one side of the river to the other
there are cables made of reeds like osiers, but as thick as
a man's thigh, and they are fastened to great stones. From
one cable to the other is the width of a cart. Smaller cords
are interwoven between the cables, and great stones are
fastened beneath, to steady them. By one of these bridges
the common people cross over, and a porter is stationed
there to receive transit dues; while the Lords and Captains
use the other, which is always closed, but they opened it
for the Captain and his followers, and the horses crossed
over very well.

The Captain rested in this village for two days, because
both men and horses were fatigued by the bad road. The
Christians were very well received, and were supplied with

[5] On this day the party crossed from the Marañon to the coast watershed.

food and all that they required. The Lord of this village was called Pumapaccha. They departed from it and came to a small village, where they were given all they wanted, and near it they crossed another bridge of network, like the former one. They passed the night two leagues further on, at another village, where the people came out to receive them as friends and gave food to the Christians, and Indians to carry their loads. This day's march was through a valley covered with maize, with villages on either side of the road. The next day was Sunday. They started in the morning, and came to a village where the Captain and his companions were well received. At night they reached another village, where the people offered sheep and chicha and all other necessaries. All this land has abundant supplies of maize and many flocks; and, as the Christians marched along the road, they saw the sheep crossing it. Next day, at dinner time, the Captain reached a great town called Huaras,[6] the Lord of which was called Pumacapllai. He and his people supplied the Christians with provisions, and with Indians to carry the loads. This town is in a plain, and a river flows near it. Other villages were in sight, with flocks and maize fields. They had two hundred head of sheep in a yard, merely to supply the wants of the Captain and his men. The Captain departed in the afternoon, and stopped for the night at another village called Sucaracoai, where he was well received. The Lord of this village was named Marcocana. Here the Captain rested for one day, because both men and horses were tired. A strict watch was kept because the village was large, and Chilicuchima was near with 55,000 men. Next day they departed from this village, and, after marching through a valley, where there was much tilled land and many flocks, stopped for the night at a distance of two leagues, in a

---

[6] Capital of the modern Department of Ancachs, in the valley of the Santa.

small village called Pachicoto. Here the Captain left the
royal road which leads to Cuzco, and took that of the coast
valley. Next day he stopped for the night at a place called
Marcara, the chief of which was named Corcara. Here
there are pastures, and at a certain time of the year they
bring the flocks to browse, as they do in Castille and
Estremadura. From this village the rivers flow to the sea,
which makes the road very difficult, for all the country in-
land is very cold, and with much water and snow. The
coast is very hot, and there is very little rain. The rain is
not sufficient for the crops, but the waters that flow from
the mountains irrigate the land, which yields abundant
supplies of provisions and fruits.

Next day they departed from this village, and marching
along the banks of a river, following its downward course
through fields and fruit gardens, they stopped for the night
at a village called Guaracanga. Next day they stopped at
a large place near the sea called Parpunga. It has a strong
house with seven encircling walls painted in many devices
both inside and outside, with portals well-built like those of
Spain, and two tigers at the principal doorway.[7] The inhabitants were filled with fear at the sight of a people never
before seen, and of the horses, which astonished them still
more. The Captain spoke to them through the interpreter
who accompanied him, to re-assure them, and they then did
good service.

In this village they came upon another broader road,
made by the people of the coast, and bounded by walls on
either side. The Captain rested for two days in this town

[7] I think this Parpunga is the *Parmonga* of Cieza de Leon (p. 247)
and the *Parmunca* of Garcilasso (ii, p. 195). Rivero spells it *Para-
manca* (p. 259). Cieza de Leon described the fortress, the ruins of
which are also mentioned by Proctor (*Travels*, p. 175). Both Cieza de
Leon and Proctor mention the paintings on the walls, alluded to in the
text, by Astete. See also *Antiguedades Peruanas*, p. 288.

of Parpunga to refresh his people and get them re-shod.
On starting again, they crossed a river in balsas, the horses
swimming. He passed the night at a village called Guamamayo,[8] which is in a ravine near the sea. Near it they
had to cross another river with great difficulty by swimming,
for it was much swollen, and flowing rapidly. They have
no bridges across these coast rivers, because they become
very wide when they are swollen. The lord of this village
and his people did good service in assisting to carry the
baggage across, and they gave very good food to the
Christians, and men to carry their loads. The Captain
and his followers set out from this village on the 9th day of
January,[9] and passed the night in another village subject to
Guamamayo, and three leagues from it by the road. The
greater part was inhabited, and there were tilled fields,
trees, fruit gardens, and a clean walled road. Next day
the Captain stopped at a very large village near the sea,
called Huara.[1] This town is well situated, and contains
large edifices for lodging. The Christians were well served
by the chiefs and the Indians, who supplied them with what
they required for the day. On the following day the
Captain stopped at a village called Llachu, to which he
gave the name of "the town of the partridges," because
there were many partridges kept in cages in all the houses.[2]
The Indians of this village were friendly and did good
service. The chief of this village did not make his appearance.

[8] This is the Huaman-mayu, or "Falcon river", mentioned by Cieza
de Leon. It is now called La Barranca. The breadth of the channel
is about a quarter of a mile, and during the rains it is completely full,
and often impassable. See also *Garcilasso*, ii, p. 185.
[9] This date must be either a misprint or a mistake of Astete. They
left Cassa-marca on Wednesday, January 5th. On the 9th they were
at Andamarca. By following their itinerary, it will be found that the
date in the text should be January 30th.
[1] The modern town and river of Huara. The port, at the mouth of
the river, is Huacho.   [2] This may be Chancay.

The Captain started rather early next morning, because he was informed that the march would be long, and he reached a large village called Suculacumbi at dinner time, a distance of five leagues. The Lord of the village and his Indians were friendly, and supplied all the food that was necessary for that day. At the hour of vespers they set out from this village, in order to reach the town where the mosque is on the next day. They crossed a great river by a ford,[3] and marched along a road with a wall on each side, passing the night at a place belonging to the town, and at a distance of a league and a half from it.[4]

The next day was Sunday, the 30th of January.[5] The Captain departed from this village, and, without leaving groves and villages,[6] he reached Pachacama, which is the town where the mosque stands. Halfway there is another village, where the Captain dined.[7] The Lord of Pachacama and the principal men came out to receive the Captain and the Christians, and showed a desire to be friends with the Spaniards. The Captain went to lodge, with his followers, in some large chambers in one part of the town.[8] He said that he had come, by order of the Governor, for the gold of that mosque, and that they were to collect it and deliver it

---

[3] The river Rimac. They must have passed over the site of the future city of Lima.

[4] Marching by the upper road, at the foot of the mountains, they came to the village of Pachacamac, some miles up the valley, with its groves of chirimoyas and *suchis* (*Plumieria*). A charming spot.

[5] This date should be Sunday, February 5th. January 30th was on a Monday.

[6] The valley of Lurin, on the left bank of the stream. The ruined city and temple are in the desert, on the right bank.

[7] Not now existing. There is a hacienda, on an isolated rock overlooking the rich vale of Lurin, called Bella Vista, half-way between the village of Pachacamac and the ruins of the city and temple.

[8] These are courts rather than chambers, of great extent, with smaller chambers and recesses opening upon them, all built of immense *adobes*. They are still standing.

up, or to convey it to where the Governor then was. All the principal men of the town and the attendants of the Idol assembled and replied that they would give it, but they continued to dissimulate and make excuses. At last they brought a very little, and said that they had no more. The Captain dissimulated also, and said that he wished to go and see the Idol they had, and he went. It was in a good house, well painted, in a very dark chamber with a close fetid smell. Here there was a very dirty Idol made of wood, and they say that this is their God who created them and sustains them, and gives them their food. At the foot of the Idol there were some offerings of gold, and it was held in such veneration that only the attendants and servants, who, as they say, were appointed by it, were allowed to officiate before it. No other person might enter, nor is any other considered worthy even to touch the walls of the house. The Captain ascertained that the Devil frequented this Idol, and spoke with his servants, saying diabolical things, which were spread over all the land. They look upon him as God, and offer many sacrifices to him. They come to this Devil, from distances of three hundred leagues, with gold and silver and cloth. Those that arrive, go to the porter and beg that their gift may be accepted. He enters and speaks with the Idol, who says that he consents. Before any of his ministers may enter to minister to him, they say that they must fast for many days and refrain from women. In all the streets of this town, and at its principal gates, and round this house, there are many wooden Idols, which they worship as imitations of their Devil. It was ascertained from many lords of this land that, from the town of Catamez,[9] which is at the commencement of this government, all the people of this coast serve this mosque with gold and silver, and offer a certain tribute every year. There were houses and superintendents to receive the

---

[9] Atacames, on the coast of Ecuador.

tribute, where they found some gold, and there were signs
that much more had been taken away. Many Indians de-
posed that the gold was removed by order of the Devil. I
omit many things that might be said touching the worship
of this Idol, to avoid prolixity. But it is believed among
the Indians that this Idol is their God, that he can destroy
them if they offend him and do not serve him well, and that
all the things in the world are in his hands. The people
were so shocked and terrified at the Captain having merely
gone in to see it, that they thought the Idol would destroy
all the Christians. But the Spaniards gave the Indians to
understand that they were in a great error, and that he who
spoke from the inside of the Idol was the Devil, who deceived them. They were told that from henceforth they
must not believe him, nor do what he advised them; and
were taught other things touching their idolatries.

The Captain ordered the vault, in which the Idol was, to
be pulled down, and the Idol to be broken before all the
people. He then told them many things touching our
Holy Catholic Faith, and he taught them the sign of the
cross ✠, that they might be able to defend themselves
against the Devil. This town of Pachacama is very large.
Adjoining the mosque there is a house of the Sun, well
built, and situated on a hill, with five surrounding walls.
There are houses with terrace roofs as in Spain. The town
appears to be old, judging from the ruined houses it contains; and the greater part of the outer wall has fallen.
The name of the principal lord is Taurichumbi. The neighbouring lords came to the town to see the Captain, with
presents of the products of their land, and with gold and
silver. They wondered greatly that the Captain should
have dared to enter where the Idol was, and to see it
broken.

The Lord of Malaque,[1] named Lincoto, came to offer

[1] Mala, a coast valley to the south of Pachacamac.

obedience to his Majesty, and brought a present of gold and silver. The Lord of Poax, named Alincai, did the same. The Lord of Gualco,[2] named Guarilli, also brought gold and silver. The Lord of Chincha,[3] with ten of his chief men, came with a present of gold and silver. This Lord said that his name was Tamviambea. The Lord of Guaxcha-paicho, and the Lord of Colixa named Aci, the Lord of Sallicaimarca named Yspilo, and other principal Lords of the surrounding country, brought in presents of gold and silver, which, joined to that taken out of the mosque, made ninety thousand *pesos*.[4] The Captain talked very kindly to all these Chiefs, rejoicing at their coming. He commanded them, in the name of his Majesty, always to behave in the same way, and dismissed them, well satisfied.

In this town of Pachacama, the Captain Hernando Pizarro received news that Chilicuchima,[5] a Captain of Atabaliba, was at a distance of four days' journey with a large force, and with the gold; and that he would not march onwards, but declared that he was ready to fight the Christians. The Captain sent a messenger to him, urging him to continue his march with the gold, as his master was in prison ; telling him that he was long behind his time, and that the Governor was angry at his delay, as he had been expected for many days. He sent many other messages, urging him to come, as he was unable to go and meet him where he then was, because the road was bad for the horses ; and arranging that the one who reached a certain village on the road first should wait there for the other. Chilicuchima

---

[2] Huarcu. The modern name of this rich valley is Cañete. It contains several flourishing sugar estates.

[3] The next valley, south of Cañete.

[4] It was said, according to Herrera, that the Priests concealed four hundred loads of gold and silver, and that Hernando Pizarro only collected nine hundred *castellanos*. Dec. v, lib. ii, cap. 3, p. 54.

[5] Chalcuchima.

sent a message in reply, saying that he would do what the Captain desired, and that he had no other intention.

The Captain then set out from the town of Pachacama, to form a junction with Chilicuchima. He marched by the same road as he had come, until he reached Huara, which is on the coast near the sea. Then he left the coast and marched into the interior. The Captain Hernando Pizarro left the town of Huara on the 3rd of March, and advanced along a road on the bank of a river during the whole day, where there were many groves of trees. He passed the night at a village on the banks of the river. The village where the Captain slept belongs to the town of Huara, and is called Guaranga. Next day the Captain left this village, and reached another called Aillon, near the mountains. It is subject to a larger place called Aratambo, which is rich in flocks and maize crops.

On the 5th of March he passed the night at a village belonging to Caxatambo, called Chincha. On the road they had to cross a pass where the snow was very deep, reaching to the girths of the horses. This village has large flocks. The Captain remained there for two days. On Saturday, the 7th of March, he set out, and passed the night at Caxatambo. This is a large town, situated in a deep valley, where there are many flocks, and all along the road there were sheepfolds. The chief of this village is called Sachao, and he did good service to the Spaniards. At this town the Captain changed his route, in order to take the broad road by which Chilicuchima would come, which entailed a flank march of three days. Here the Captain made inquiries whether Chilicuchima had passed, in order to form a junction. All the Indians said that he had passed with the gold; but it afterwards appeared that they had been told to say this, that the Captain might be induced to march onwards; while he remained in Xauxa, with no intention of moving. The Captain, however, considered that these

Indians seldom spoke the truth ; so he determined, although it entailed great trouble and danger, to march to the royal road by which Chilicuchima must go, in order to ascertain whether he had already passed. If he had not gone on, the Captain resolved to seek him out, wherever he might be, as well to secure the gold as to disperse his army.

The Captain, with his followers, took the way leading to a large village called Pombo, which is on the royal road. On Monday, the 9th of March, they slept at a village, situated amongst mountains, called Diu. The chief of this village was friendly, and gave the Christians all they required for the night. The Governor started early next morning, and passed the following night in a small village of shepherds, near a lake of sweet water, about three leagues in circuit ;[6] on a plain where there were large flocks of sheep with very fine wool. Next day, which was Wednesday, in the morning, the Captain and his companions reached the village of Pombo,[7] and the Lords of Pombo came out to meet him, with some Captains of Ataliba who were there with troops. Here the Captain found one hundred and fifty *arrobas* of gold, which Chilicuchima had sent, while he himself remained with his forces in Xauxa. When the Captain had taken up his quarters, he asked the Captains how it was that Chilicuchima had sent that gold, and had not come himself according to orders. They answered that it was because he was in great fear of the Christians, and also because he was waiting for more gold that was coming from Cuzco, as he did not like to come himself with so little.

The Captain Hernando Pizarro sent a messenger from this village to Chilicuchima, to let him know that as he had

---

[6] This seems to have been the lake of Lauricocha, the source of the Marañon.

[7] Pumpu of Garcilasso de la Vega, the modern Bombon.

not come, he would go to him, and that he need have no
fear. The Captain rested for one day in that village to
refresh the horses, in case it should be necessary to fight.
On Friday, the 14th of March, the Captain set out from the
village of Pombo, with his horse and foot, to go to Xauxa.
That night was passed in a village called Xacamalca, six
leagues from Pombo, over level ground. On this plain
there is a lake of sweet water which commences near this
village, and has a circuit of eight or ten leagues.[8] The lake
has villages all round its shores, and large flocks, while in
its waters are birds and small fish.[9] The father of Atabaliba
had many *balsas* in this lake, which were brought from
Tumbez for his amusement. A river flows out of the lake
to the village of Pombo, and a branch of it is very deep and
rapid. They can float by it to a bridge near the village;
and those who pass pay dues as in Spain. All along the
banks of this river there are large flocks, and the name of
Guadiana was given to it, because of the resemblance to
that river in Spain.

On Saturday, the 15th of the month, the Captain left the
village of Xacamalca, and after marching three leagues he
came to a house, where he and his men were well supplied
with food. He passed that night three leagues further on,
at a town called Tarma, which is on the slope of a mountain.
Here he was lodged in a painted house, which contained
good rooms. The chief of this place behaved well, both
in supplying food and men to carry loads. On Sunday
morning the Captain set out rather early from this village,

[8] The lake of Bombon or Chinchay-cocha. It is thirty-six miles long,
by six broad, and 12,940 feet above the sea. The plain or basin in
which it lies is forty-five miles long. The river of Xauxa flows out of
the lake.

[9] A great number of large and beautiful water fowl, including the
scarlet flamingo, and several varieties of snipe, frequent the banks of
the lake, which are overgrown with reeds. See *Von Tschudi* and
Herndon.

having a long march before him. He caused his men to advance in order of battle, because he suspected some treachery, not having received any answer from Chilicuchima. At the hour of vespers he reached a village called Yanaimalca, where the people came out to him. Here he received news that Chilicuchima was not in Xauxa, which increased his suspicions. The Captain was now only a league from Xauxa, so after dinner he again marched onwards, and, having come in sight of the town, he saw many bodies of men from a hill; but he could not make out whether they were soldiers or townspeople who had assembled for some festival.

As soon as the Captain arrived, and before he dismounted, he asked for Chilicuchima, and the people answered that he was at some other village, and that he would return next day. He had absented himself on pretence of business until he might learn from the Indians who came with the Captain the intentions of the Spaniards; for he saw that he had committed a fault in not having kept his promise, and that the Captain had come eighty leagues in pursuit of him. These considerations made him think that the Spaniards came to seize or kill him, and he had absented himself from fear of them, especially of those who were on horseback. The Captain had with him a son of the old Cuzco who, when he heard of the absence of Chilicuchima, said that he wished to go where he was, and set out in a litter. All that night the horses were saddled and bridled, and the Lords of the town were told that no Indian was to appear in the square, because the horses were angry and would kill them. Next day that son of the Cuzco returned with Chilicuchima, both in litters, and numerously attended. On entering the square they alighted, and, leaving all their servants, they went on foot, with a few attendants, to the house occupied by the Captain Hernando Pizarro, for Chilicuchima to see him and offer his excuses for not having fulfilled his promise, or come out to receive him. He said his business had prevented him from doing more. The Captain asked why he had not come to meet him, as he had promised. Chilicuchima answered that his master Atabaliba had sent orders to him to remain where he was. The Captain then said that he felt no anger against him, but that he must accompany him back to the Governor, who had his master Atabaliba a prisoner, and who would keep him until he had given up the gold that had been demanded. The Captain added that he knew how much gold there was, and that it must be delivered up, but he assured Chilicuchima that, although he must accompany him back, he would be well treated. Chilicuchima replied that his Lord had sent to order him to do otherwise, and not to go, because that country was lately conquered, and might again rebel if he left it. Hernando Pizarro conversed with him for some time, and finally it was arranged that they should pass the night there, and again discuss the matter in the morning. The Captain desired to carry his point by fair means, because he was anxious to avoid disturbances, lest it should compromise the safety of three Spaniards who had gone to the city of Cuzco. Next morning Chilicuchima came to the Captain's lodging and said that, as he desired him to accompany the Spaniards, he could not refuse to obey, and that he was ready to go, leaving another Captain with the troops at Xauxa. On that day he got together about thirty loads of gold; and after marching for two days they met thirty or forty loads. During those days the Spaniards kept a good look out, the horses being kept saddled night and day; for this Captain of Atabaliba had so large a force that if he had made a night attack on the Spaniards he would have done much mischief.

The town of Xauxa is very large. It is situated in a beautiful valley, and enjoys a temperate climate. A very large river flows near the town. The land is fertile. The town is built like those of Spain, with regular streets, and many subject villages are in sight.   The town and district are very populous, and the Spaniards saw one hundred thousand people assemble every day in the principal square. The market places and streets were also crowded.   There were men whose duty it was to count all these people, and to know who came in for the service of the troops ; and other men had to watch and take note of all who entered the town.   Chilicuchima had stewards whose duty it was to supply provisions, and many carpenters who worked in wood, and many other men to attend upon his wants and wait on his person.   There were three or four porters in his house, and both in his household service, and in everything else he imitated his Lord.   He was feared throughout this land, for he was a brave warrior, and, under orders from his Lord, he had conquered more than two hundred leagues of country, and had had many encounters both in the plains and in the passes, in all of which he had been victorious, and in none had he been vanquished throughout all that land.

On Friday, the 20th of March, the Captain Hernando Pizarro departed from that city of Xauxa to return to Caxamalca, accompanied by Chilicuchima.   He marched by the same road to the village of Pompo, where he stayed for the day he arrived, and one more.   On Wednesday he set out from this village of Pompo, and marching over plains covered with flocks, he passed the night at some large buildings.   On that day it snowed heavily.   Next day he came to a village amongst the mountains called Tambo, which is near a large and deep river, where there is a bridge.   There is a flight of stone steps to descend to the river, and if the position was defended, much mischief might be done.   The Captain received good service from the Lord of this village, and was supplied with all that he and his party required. They made a great festival out of respect for the Captain

Hernando Pizarro, and because Chilicuchima accompanied him. Next day they came to a village called Tomsucancha, the lord of which, named Tillima, received them well. There were plenty of Indians fit for service; for, though the village was small, many had assembled from the surrounding country to see the Spaniards. In this village there are small sheep with very fine wool, like those of Spain. Next day they reached a village called Guaneso,[1] a march of five leagues, the greater part over a paved road, with channels of water by the side. They say that the road was paved on account of the snow, which, at a certain season of the year, falls over that land. This town of Guaneso is large. It is situated in a valley, surrounded by steep mountains, the valley being three leagues in circuit. On the side leading to Caxamalca there is a long and very steep ascent. The Captain and his followers were very well received, and during the two days that they remained, the inhabitants celebrated several feasts. This town has other surrounding villages under its jurisdiction. It is a land of many flocks.

On the last day of March the Captain departed from this town, and reached a bridge over a large river, built of very stout timber. There were guards stationed there to receive transit dues, as is their custom. They passed the night at a distance of four leagues from the town, where Chilicuchima had caused all necessary preparations to be made. Next day, being the 1st of April, they reached a village called Piscomarca. It is on the slope of a very steep mountain. Its chief is named Parpay. Next day the Captain departed from this village, and, after a march of three leagues, arrived at a good village called Huari,[2] where there is a large and deep river, over which there is another bridge. This position is very strong, there being deep ravines on either flank. Chilicuchima said that here he had fought a battle with the troops of the Cuzco, who guarded the pass, defending

---

[1] Huanuco.   [2] In the valley of the Marañon.

it for two or three days. When those of Cuzco were defeated, and some of their enemies had crossed the river,
they destroyed the bridge, so that Chilicuchima and his
troops swam across, and killed many of the men of Cuzco.

Next day the Captain set out, and, after a march of five
leagues, he passed the night at a village called Guacango.
Next day he reached the large town of Piscobamba,[8] which
is on the side of a mountain. The chief is called Tauquame;
and he and his people received the Captain well, and did
good service to his followers. Half-way to this town, at
Huacacamba, there is another deep river with two bridges
of net-work close together, resting on a foundation of stone
rising from the water; like those I have mentioned before.
From one side to the other there are cables of reed, the
size of a man's thigh, and between are woven many stout
cords; to which large stones are fastened, for the purpose
of steadying the bridge. The horses crossed this bridge
without trouble; but it is a nervous thing to pass over it
for the first time, though there is no danger, as it is very
strong. There are guards at all these bridges, as in Spain.
Next day the Captain departed from Piscobamba, and
reached some buildings, after a march of five leagues. Next
day he came to a village called Agoa, which is subject to
Piscobamba. It is a good village among the mountains, and
is surrounded by fields of maize. The chief and his people
supplied what was required for the night, and next morning
provided porters for the baggage. Next day the Captain
marched for four leagues over a very rugged road, and
passed the night at Conchuco.[4] This village is in a hollow.
Half a league before reaching it, there is a wide road cut in

[3] See *Cieza de Leon*, p. 293. He says that Piscobamba is eight leagues
from Huaraz, over very rugged mountains. See also *Garcilasso de la
Vega*, ii, p. 134.

[4] See *Cieza de Leon*, p. 286. It is the Cunchucu of *Garcilasso*, ii, p.
134.

steps in the rock, and there are many difficult passes, and
places which might easily be defended.   Next day they set
out, and reached a place called Andamarca, which is the
point where they had diverged to go to Pachacama.   At
this town the two royal roads to Cuzco unite.[5]   From Andamarca to Pombo[6] there are three leagues over a very
rugged road ; and stone steps are cut for the ascents and
descents ; while on the outer side there is a stone wall, to protect the traveller from the danger of slipping.   If any man
fell, he would be dashed to pieces ; and it is an excellent
thing for the horses, as they would fall if there was no
flanking wall.   In the middle of the road there is a bridge
of stone and wood, very well built, between two masses of
rock.   At one end of the bridge there are well-built lodgings
and a paved court, where, according to the Indians, the
lords of the land had banquets and feasts when they travelled
by that road.

From this place the Captain Hernando Pizarro went by
the same stages as he came, until he reached the city of
Caxamalca, which he entered, with Chilicuchima, on the
25th of May,[7] 1533.   Here a thing was seen that had never
been witnessed before since the Indies were discovered.
When Chilicuchima passed through the gates of the place
where his master was imprisoned, he took a light load from
one of the Indian porters and put it on his back, an example
which was followed by many chiefs who accompanied him.
Thus laden, he and the others entered where their Lord was ;
and when Chilicuchima saw him, he raised his hands to the
Sun, and gave thanks that he had been permitted to enjoy
the sight.   Then, with much reverence, and weeping, he

---

[5] One leading, by Huaras, to the coast road at Parmunca ; the other
being the *sierra* road to Cuzco, by Xauxa.

[6] The modern Pomabamba.

[7] This should be April. At p. 90, March is given as the date. These
are probably misprints.

approached his Lord, and kissed his face, hands, and feet. The other chiefs, his companions, did the same. Atabaliba maintained a mien so majestic that, though there was not a man in the kingdom that he loved more than Chilicuchima, he did not look in his face or take more notice of him than of the vilest Indians that came into his presence. This taking up of a load to enter the presence of Atabaliba is a ceremony which was performed for all the Lords who have reigned in that land. I, Miguel de Estete, the overseer, who went on the journey that the Captain Hernando Pizarro undertook, now give this account of all that happened.

MIGUEL ESTETE.

THE FIRST AUTHOR CONTINUES.

The masters of the six ships which were at the port of San Miguel, being unable to maintain their crews, had requested the Governor to pay and despatch them. The Governor called a Council for the purpose of making the necessary arrangements and for reporting what had happened to his Majesty. It was decided that all the gold should be melted down which had been brought to Caxamalca by order of Atabaliba, as well as all that might arrive before the melting was finished. As soon as it was melted and distributed, the Governor would not be detained any longer, but would proceed to form a settlement, in obedience to the orders of his Majesty.

The publication of this resolution and the commencement of the melting took place on the 3rd of May, 1533. After ten days one of three Christians who went to the city of Cuzco arrived. He was the public notary, and he reported that that city of Cuzco had been taken possession of in the name of his Majesty. He also gave an account of the road, on which he said there were thirty principal towns, without counting Cuzco, and many other small villages. He said that Cuzco was as large as had been reported, and that it is situated on a hill side near a plain ; that the streets were very regularly arranged and paved, and that in the eight days that he had been there he had not been able to see everything. He saw a well-built house entirely plated with gold, quadrangular, and measuring three hundred and fifty paces from corner to corner. Of these gold plates they took down seven hundred, which together weighed 500 *pesos*. From another house the Indians pulled off a quantity weighing 200,000 *pesos*; but, as it was much alloyed, having but seven or eight carats the *peso*, they would not receive it. Besides these two, they did not see any other houses plated with gold; but the Indians did not permit them to see all the city. They judged from what they did see that it was very rich. They found the Captain Quizquiz in the city, holding it for Atabaliba with a garrison of thirty thousand men, because it is threatened by Caribs[8] and other tribes who wage war against that city. He reported many other things that there were in Cuzco, and that it was well ordered, and that a chief was coming with the other two Spaniards with seven hundred plates of gold and much silver that was delivered to the chief at Xauxa, left behind by Chilicuchima. The whole quantity of gold collected by them was one hundred and seventy-eight loads, and these loads were in *paliqueres*,[9] each borne by four Indians. They were bringing little silver, and the gold was

[8] The Spaniards had very hazy ideas about the Caribs; they used the word as a vague term to apply to any Indians in arms, of whom they knew nothing. The garrison at Cuzco, commanded by Quizquiz, was no doubt threatened by the defeated, but still faithful, troops of the legitimate Ynca.

[9] This is not a Spanish word. Ternaux Compans thinks that the word means a litter ; perhaps a corruption of the Indian word *palkee* or *palanquin;* which may have come into use through the Portuguese.

delivered to the Christians by little and little, and slowly,
because it was necessary to employ many Indians, who had
to go from village to village to collect it. He calculated
that the gold which was on the road would arrive at Caxamalca in about a month. It actually arrived on the 13th
of June, and consisted of two hundred loads of gold and
twenty-five of silver. The gold appeared to be of more
than one hundred and thirty carats. After the arrival of
this first instalment another sixty loads of less fine gold
came in. The greater part was in plates, like the boards of
a box, and three to four *palmos* in length. These had been
taken from the walls of the house, and they had holes in
them, showing that they had been secured by nails. They
completed the founding and partitioning of all this gold and
silver on the day of Santiago, the gold and silver being
weighed by a *Romana*.[1] The account was then taken, all
being reduced to good gold ; and it was found to make a
total of 326,539 *pesos* of good gold.[2] After deducting the
fees of the founder, the Royal fifth amounted to 262,259
pesos of pure gold. Of the silver there were 51,610 *marcs*,
of which 10,121 *marcs* of silver formed the Royal fifth.[3] All
the rest, after the Royal fifths and the fees of the founder
had been deducted, was divided amongst all the conquerors
who accompanied the Governor. The horsemen each received 8,880 *pesos* of gold and 362 *marcs* of silver.[4] The
foot soldiers each had 4,440 *pesos*, and 181 *marcs* of silver,
some more and some less, according as the Governor considered that each man deserved reward, with reference to

[1] A steelyard.

[2] The Governor's own share was 200,000 *pesos* of gold and 50,000 in
silver, besides the gold litter of Atahuallpa.

[3] Garcilasso gives the royal fifth at 546,250 *pesos* of gold and 105,750
pesos of silver.

[4] Garcilasso says that the shares of these captains of cavalry was
90,000 *pesos* of gold and 30,000 of silver. The sixty men had 726,000
pesos of gold and 180,000 in silver.

his services, position, and the labours he had gone through.[5]
A certain quantity of gold, which was set apart by the
Governor before the partition took place, was given to the
citizens of San Miguel, to those who came with the Captain
Diego de Almagro,[6] and to all the merchants and sailors
who arrived afterwards. Thus everyone in the country received something; so that it might be called a general
melting, as it was general to all.[7] One remarkable thing in

[5] Four captains of infantry got 90,000 *pesos* of gold and 30,000 of
silver, and a hundred men got 900,000 *pesos* of gold and 135,000 of
silver.

[6] Almagro got 30,000 *pesos* of gold and 10,000 of silver.
    The value of the silver was reckoned at twenty per cent. of the gold.
A ducat was worth eleven rials and one maravedi, or 375 maravedis.
100 *pesos* of gold were equal to 120 of silver, and 120 *pesos* of silver
were equal to 144 ducats. Therefore, 100 *pesos* of gold = 144 ducats.

			Ducats.
The Governor's share of gold	- - - -		252,000
,, ,, silver	- - -		60,000
Three Captains of Cavalry. Share of gold			129,600
,, ,, ,, silver		-	36,000
Four Captains of Infantry ,, gold	-	-	129,600
,, ,, ,, silver		-	36,000
Sixty horsemen - ,, gold	-		1,036,800
,, - - ,, silver		-	129,600
Hundred foot soldiers - ,, gold	-	-	1,296,000
,, ,, - ,, silver		-	162,000
The 240 men of Almagro ,, gold	-	-	259,200
,, ,, - ,, silver		-	72,000
The Captain Almagro - ,, gold	-	-	43,200
,, ,, - ,, silver		-	12,000
The Royal Fifth - ,, gold	-		786,600
,, ,, - ,, silver		-	126,900
Increase of the refined silver	- - -		38,170
Total ransom of Atahuallpa	-	-	4,605,670

Of this sum 3,933,000 ducats was the value of the gold, and 672,670
ducats the value of the silver. This may be considered equal to
£3,500,000 of our money. (*G. de la Vega*, Pt. II, lib. i, cap. 38, p. 51.)
    In the division of plunder our author, Francisco de Xeres, as a horse-

this melting was that on one day they melted 80,000 *pesos*. Usually the quantity was 50,000 to 60,000 *pesos* a day. The melting was done by the Indians, who have among them good silversmiths and melters, and they worked with nine forges.

I must not omit to mention the prices which have been given for provisions and other goods in this country, though some are so high as to be incredible. Yet I can say with truth that I saw it, and that I bought some of the things. A horse was sold for 2,500 *pesos*, and another for 3,300 *pesos*. The ordinary price of horses was 2,500 *pesos*, and they were difficult to get at that price. A jar of wine, of three *azumbres*, sold for sixty *pesos*. I gave forty *pesos* for two *azumbres*. A pair of high boots fetched thirty or forty *pesos*, and a pair of shoes as much ; a cloak one hundred to one hundred and twenty *pesos* ; a sword forty to fifty ; a string of garlics half a *peso*. All other things werè in proportion. (A *peso* is as much as a *castellano*.) A sheet of paper sold for ten *pesos*. I gave twelve *pesos* for half an ounce of damaged saffron. Much more might be said of the high prices at which everything was sold ; and of the little store that was set by gold and silver. If one man owed anything to another, he paid it in a lump of gold, without weighing the gold, and being quite indifferent whether it was worth double the amount of the debt or not. Those who owed money went from house to house, followed by an Indian laden with gold, and seeking out their creditors to pay them.

Having related how the melting and distributing of the gold and silver were finished, the wealth of the land, and how little store was set by gold and silver, as well by Spaniards as Indians, I will now say something of the place which

man, received 362 *marcos* of silver and 8880 *pesos* of gold ; besides 94 *marcos* and 2220 *pesos*, to be divided between himself and Pedro Sancho for Secretary's work.

was subject to the Cuzco, and now belongs to Atabaliba.[8] They say that it contained two houses made of gold, and that the straws with which it was roofed were all made of gold. With the gold that was brought from Cuzco, there were some straws made of solid gold, with their spikes, just as they would grow in the fields. If I was to recount all the different varieties in the shape of the pieces of gold, my story would never end. There was a stool of gold that weighed eight *arrobas*.[9] There were great fountains with their pipes, through which water flowed into a reservoir on the same fountains, where there were birds of different kinds, and men drawing water from the fountain, all made of gold. It was also ascertained from Atabaliba and Chilicuchima, and many others, that in Xauxa Atabaliba had sheep and shepherds tending them, all made of gold; and the sheep and shepherds were large, and of the size that they are met with in this land. These pieces belonged to his father, and he promised to give them to the Spaniards. They relate wonderful things of the wealth of Atabaliba and his father.

Now I must mention a thing which should not be forgotten. A chief, who was Lord of Caxamalca, appeared before the Governor and said to him through the interpreters: "I would have you to know that, after Atabaliba was taken prisoner, he sent to Quito, his native land, and to all the other provinces, with orders to collect troops to march against you and your followers, and to kill you all; and all these troops are coming under the command of a great captain called Lluminabi.[1] This army is now very near to this place. It will come at night and attack the

---

[8] The city of Cuzco.

[9] The *tiana* or throne of the Yncas. It fell to the share of Francisco Pizarro himself. According to Garcilasso it was worth 25,000 *pesos* of gold. (II, lib. i, cap. 38.)

[1] Rumi-ñaui, a general of Atahuallpa. The word means "Stone-eyed."

camp, setting fire in all directions, and the first they will try to kill will be yourself, and they will deliver Atabaliba out of his prison. From Quito are coming two hundred thousand men of war, and thirty thousand Caribs who eat human flesh ; and from another province called Paçalta, and from other parts, come a great number of soldiers."

When the Governor heard this, he thanked the chief and did him much honour, and sent for a clerk to put it all down. Then he made further inquiries, and, having taken the statement to an uncle of Atabaliba, to some principal chiefs, and to some women, he found that all that the chief of Caxamalca had said was true.

The Governor then spoke to Atabaliba, saying : " What treason is this that you have prepared for me ? For me who have treated you with honour, like a brother, and have trusted in your words !" Then he told him all the information he had received. Atabaliba answered, saying : " Are you laughing at me ? You are always making jokes when you speak to me. What am I, and all my people, that we should trouble such valiant men as you are ? Do not talk such nonsense to me." He said all this without betraying a sign of anxiety ; but he laughed the better to conceal his evil design, and practised many other arts such as would suggest themselves to a quick-witted man. After he was a prisoner, the Spaniards who heard him were astounded to find so much wisdom in a barbarian. The Governor ordered a chain to be brought, which was fastened round the neck of Atabaliba. He then sent two Indians as spies to find out where this army was, for it was reported to be only seven leagues from Caxamalca. He wished to ascertain whether it was in such a position as that a hundred cavalry could be sent against it. But it was reported that the enemy was posted in a very rugged position, and that he was approaching nearer. As soon as the chains were put upon Atabaliba he had sent a messenger to his great

Captain saying that the Governor had killed him, and on receiving this news the Captain and his army began to retreat. But Atabaliba sent other messengers after the first, ordering them to advance without delay, and sending orders how and in what direction to march, and at what hour to attack the camp; adding that he was still alive, but that if they delayed he would be killed.

The Governor knew all this, and he ordered a careful watch to be kept in the camp. The cavalry were to go the rounds three times during the night; fifty horsemen going each round, and at the rounds of daybreak the whole hundred and fifty horsemen. During these nights the Governor and his Captains never slept, but looked after the rounds, and saw that all were on the alert. The soldiers who slept during the watch did not let go their arms, and their horses were kept saddled. This watchfulness was continued in the camp until, at sunset one Saturday evening two Indians, of those who served the Spaniards, came in and reported that they had fled from the hostile army, which was only three leagues distant, and that on that or the next night the camp of the Christians would be attacked; because they were marching rapidly in obedience to orders from Atabaliba.

Then the Governor, with the concurrence of the officers of his Majesty, and of the captains and persons of experience, sentenced Atabaliba to death.[2] His sentence was that, for the treason he had committed, he should die by burning, unless he became a Christian; and this execution was for the security of the Christians, the good of the whole land, and to secure its conquest and pacification. For on the death of Atabaliba all his troops would presently dis-

---

[2] " Atabalipa wept, and said that they should not kill him, that there was not an Indian in the land who would move without his orders, and that, he being prisoner, what could they fear? I saw the Marquis weep with sorrow, at not being able to spare his life, by reason of the risk of his escaping."—*Pedro Pizarro.*

perse, and would not have the courage to attack us or to obey his orders.

They brought out Atabaliba to execution; and, when he came into the square, he said he would become a Christian. The Governor was informed, and ordered him to be baptized. The ceremony was performed by the very reverend Father Friar Vicente de Valverde. The Governor then ordered that he should not be burnt, but that he should be fastened to a pole in the open space and strangled. This was done, and the body was left until the morning of the next day, when the Monks, and the Governor with the other Spaniards, conveyed it into the church, where it was interred with much solemnity, and with all the honours that could be shown it.[3]

---

[3] The pretext for murdering Atahuallpa was false, and Xeres, the murderer's secretary, knew that it was false when he wrote this narrative. It was pretended that an Indian army was assembled at Huamachuco, and Hernando de Soto, who was a gentleman and no murderer, was sent, with a small force, ostensibly to ascertain the truth of the report, but really to get him out of the way. He was accompanied by Rodrigo Orgoñez, Pedro Ortiz de Orue, Miguel de Estete, and Lope Velez. Hernando Pizarro had already departed for Spain, to report the discovery and with good store of gold.

Then Pizarro, Almagro, and the worst of the gang, with Friar Valverde, determined to murder Atahuallpa, and thus get rid of an obstacle in their way. There was a mock trial. Pizarro and Almagro were the Judges, the Clerk of the Court was Sancho de Cuellar, and Filipillo, who had a malignant spite against Atahuallpa, was interpreter. The indictment was drawn up in the form of twelve questions :—

1. Did you know Huayna Ccapac, and how many wives had he ?
2. Was Huascar the legitimate heir, and Atahuallpa a bastard?
3. Had the Ynca other sons?
4. Was Atahuallpa the heir by inheritance, or usurpation?
5. Was Huascar deprived by his father's will, or was he declared heir?
6. Was Huascar murdered by order of Atahuallpa ?
7. Was Atahuallpa an idolater, and did he enforce human sacrifices?
8. Had Atahuallpa waged unjust wars ?
9. Had Atahuallpa many concubines?
10. Had Atahuallpa received and spent tribute, since the arrival of the Spaniards ?

Such was the end of this man, who had been so cruel. He died with great fortitude, and without shewing any feeling, saying that he entrusted his children to the Governor.

11. Had Atahuallpa given treasure to his relations and captains, since the Spaniards came?
12. Had Atahuallpa ordered troops to be assembled to make war on the Spaniards?

Ten witnesses were examined, seven of whom were servants of the Spaniards, and Filipillo turned their words into what meaning he pleased. One witness, a captain named Quespi, suspected the interpreter, and would only answer *Ari* (Yes) and *Manan* (No), nodding and shaking his head, that all might understand.

The few men of honour and respectability, then at Caxamarca, protested against the murder. Their names are more worthy of remembrance than those of the thirteen who crossed the line at the isle of Gallo. They were: besides, 1. Hernando de Soto.

2. Francisco de Chaves,⎫ brothers, natives
3. Diego de Chaves,   ⎭   of Truxillo.
4. Francisco de Fuentes.
5. Pedro de Ayala.
6. Diego de Mora.
7. Francisco Moscoso.
8. Hernando de Haro.
9. Pedro de Mendoza.
10. Juan de Herrada.
11. Alonzo de Avila.
12. Blas de Atienza.

They represented that Pizarro had no jurisdiction over a foreign king, like Atahuallpa ; that to kill a king who was a prisoner, and whose ransom they had taken, would bring shame and dishonour on the Spanish name; that if he had done wrong the Emperor should judge him ; and they appealed from the iniquitous sentence to the justice of the Emperor, naming Juan de Herrada, one of their number, as the protector of the king Atahuallpa. But they were overruled, and the murder was perpetrated. Two days afterwards Hernando de Soto returned, and reported that there was no Indian army near, and no insurrection. He found the Governor, by way of mourning, wearing a great felt hat slouched over his eyes. He was justly indignant at the murder ; which Pizarro was unable to defend. He said : " Sir, you have done ill. It would have been right to have waited for our return; for the accusation against Atabaliba is false; no armed men have been assembled." The Governor answered : "Now I see that I have been deceived." Pizarro blamed

When they took his body to be buried there was loud mourning among the women and servants of his household. He died on Saturday, at the same hour that he was taken

Valverde the Monk, and Riquelme the Royal Treasurer, who, he said, had urged him to commit the crime ; and there were mutual recriminations.

Soon afterwards, when the Spaniards left Cassamarca and were marching on Cuzco, Titu Atauchi, the brother of Atahuallpa, attacked them at Tocto, in the province of Huayllas, with six thousand men, and captured eight Spaniards. Among his prisoners were Sancho de Cuellar, Francisco de Chaves, Hernando de Haro, Alonzo de Alarcon, and others. The Ynca Prince took them to Cassamarca, which place had then been abandoned by the Spaniards. Cuellar, who had been Clerk to the Court at the mock trial of Atahuallpa, got his deserts. He was publicly executed in the square of Cassamarca, at the same pole against which the Ynca was strangled. Alarcon, whose leg was broken, was carefully tended ; while Chaves and Haro, who had protested against the murder of Atahuallpa, were treated with the greatest kindness by the Indians. Prince Titu Atauchi made a treaty with them, in which it was stipulated that the Spaniards and Indians should be friends, that Manco (the legitimate son of Huayna Ccapac) should succeed to the *llautu* and that all the Ynca laws in favour of the people, which were not opposed to Christianity, should be observed. He then set Chaves and his comrades free, with many good wishes; and they went to Cuzco to try to get the treaty ratified by Pizarro, but without success. Titu Atauchi, who was a brave, generous, and able Prince, unfortunately died very soon afterwards.

It would be interesting to trace the fate of the twelve honourable men who protested against the murder of Atahuallpa.

Hernando de Soto, as is well known, abandoned Peru and its cruel conquerors, discovered Florida, and found a grave in the bed of the Mississippi.

Francisco de Chaves, a native of Truxillo, was afterwards employed in reducing the Conchucos. He was murdered at Lima in 1541, in attempting to defend the staircase against the assassins of Pizarro. Zarate says that when he died he was the most important personage in Peru, next to Pizarro.—*Hist. del Peru,* lib. iv, cap. 8.

Diego de Mora settled at the new city, called Truxillo, on the coast of Peru. Gasca made him a Captain of Cavalry, and we last hear of him as receiving the appointment of Corregidor of Lima, for the Royal Audience, during the rebellion of Giron.

Juan de Herrada was a staunch follower of Almagro. When that Captain made his expedition to Chile, his intimate friend Herrada was

prisoner and defeated. Some said that it was for his sins
that he died on the day and hour that he was seized. Thus
he was punished for the great evils and cruelties that he
had inflicted upon his vassals; for all, with one voice, de-
clare that he was the greatest and most cruel butcher that
had been seen among men; that for a very slight cause he
would destroy a village, such as some trivial fault committed by a single man ; and that he killed ten thousand

left behind at Cuzco, to bring reinforcements. Five months afterwards
Herrada set out with more men, and, after enduring terrible hardships,
reached Copiapo in Chile, returning with Almagro by the desert of
Atacama. He conveyed to Almagro the Royal Provision, which granted
that Captain one hundred leagues of country beyond the jurisdiction of
Pizarro. This Provision was brought out from Spain by Hernando
Pizarro, and the dispute as to the position of the frontier line led to the
civil war and the death of Almagro.

Blas de Atienza is enumerated by Balboa as one of the heroic adven-
turers who crossed the line with Pizarro at the Isle of Gallo. (See note,
p. 9.) He afterwards settled at Truxillo, on the Peruvian coast. But
we hear of him in still earlier days. When Vasco Nuñez came in sight
of the South Sea in 1513, he sent out three scouting parties to explore,
under Francisco Pizarro, Juan de Escaray, and Alonzo Martin. The
latter found a canoe on the beach, and, stepping into it, called his men
to witness that he was the first European who ever embarked on the
South Sea. His example was followed by Blas de Atienza, who cried
out that he was the second. (*Herrera*, Dec. i, lib. x, cap. 2.) His
daughter Inez de Atienza, the widow of Pedro de Arcos of Piura, was
beloved by Pedro de Ursua, whom she accompanied on his expedition to
discover El Dorado and Omagua in 1560. After his murder she became
the mistress of Lorenzo Salduendo, one of the pirates, and was herself
murdered by the notorious pirate Aguirre. (See *Search for El Dorado*,
p. 85.) A certain Friar Blas de Atienza published a book at Lima, en-
titled *Relacion de los Religiosos*, in 1617 ; and there was a Missionary
named Juan de Atienza, who died at Lima in 1592. These were probably sons of the Conqueror and brothers of the lady Inez. (*Sol del
Nuevo Mundo*, p. 59.)

I have not been able to discover the subsequent history of any of the
other denouncers of the murder of Atahuallpa. Except Francisco de
Chaves, Francisco de Fuentes, and Pedro de Mendoza, I find none in
the list of first conquerors who received shares of Atahuallpa's ransom,
so that the rest must have come with Almagro.

persons, and held all the country by tyranny, so that he was very heartily detested by all the inhabitants.

Soon afterwards the Governor took another son of old Cuzco, named Atabaliba, who had shown a desire to be friendly to the Spaniards, and placed him in the lordship, in presence of the chiefs and lords of the surrounding districts, and of many other Indians.[4] He ordered them to receive him as their lord, and to obey him as they had obeyed Atabaliba; for that he was their proper lord, being legitimate son of old Cuzco. They all answered that they would receive him as their lord, and obey him as the Governor had ordered.

Now I wish to mention a notable thing. It is, that twenty days before this happened, and before there were any tidings of the army that Atabaliba had ordered to be assembled, it happened that Atabaliba was, one night, very cheerful with some Spaniards with whom he was conversing. Suddenly there appeared a sign in the heavens, in the direction of Cuzco, like a fiery comet, which lasted during the greater part of the night. When Atabaliba saw this sign he said that a great lord would very soon have to die in that land.[5]

When the Governor had placed the younger Atabaliba in the state and lordship of that land (as we have mentioned) the Governor told him that he must communicate to him the orders of his Majesty, and what he must do to become his vassal. Atabaliba replied that he must retire during four days, without speaking to anyone, for such was the

---

[4] Herrera says he was a son of Atahuallpa, named Toparpa. But this is not an Ynca name at all. He died soon afterwards. (Dec. v, lib. iii, cap. 5, p. 59.)

[5] Garcilasso says it was a greenish-black comet, nearly as thick as a man. It was seen in July or August, 1533, and is certainly the one observed by Appian, according to Humboldt. On July 21st, 1533, standing high in the north, near the constellation of Perseus, it represented the sword which Perseus holds in his right hand.

custom among them when a Lord died, that his successor might be feared and obeyed, and afterwards all yield obedience to him. So he was in retirement for four days, and afterwards the Governor arranged conditions of peace with him, to the sound of trumpets, and the royal standard was put into his hands. He received and held it up for the Emperor our Lord, thus becoming his vassal. Then all the principal lords and chiefs, who were present, joyfully received him as their lord, kissed his hand and cheek, and, turning their faces to the sun, gave thanks with joined hands, for having been granted a native ruler. Thus was this lord received in the place of Atabaliba, and presently he put on a very rich fringe, secured round his head and descending over the forehead, so as almost to cover his eyes. Among these people this is the crown which he who is Lord of the lordship of Cuzco wears, and so it was worn by Atabaliba.

After all this, some of the Spaniards who had conquered the land, chiefly those who had been there a long time, and others who were worn out with illness or unable to serve by reason of their wounds, besought leave from the Governor to depart with the gold, silver, and precious stones that had fallen to their share, and to return to their homes. Permission was granted, and some of them went with Hernando Pizarro, the brother of the Governor. Others received permission afterwards, seeing that new men continued to resort to this land, drawn thither by the fame of its riches. The Governor gave some sheep and Indians to the Spaniards who had obtained leave to go home, to carry their gold and silver and clothes to the town of San Miguel. On the road some of them lost gold and silver to the amount of more than 25,000 *castellanos*, because the sheep ran away with the gold and silver, and some of the Indians also fled. On this journey they suffered much hunger and thirst, and many hardships from a want of people to carry their loads.

From the city of Cuzco to the port the distance is nearly two hundred leagues. At last they embarked and went to Panama, and thence to Nombre de Dios, where they again embarked, and our Lord conducted them to Seville, at which port four ships have arrived, up to the present time, which brought the following quantity of gold and silver :—

On the 5th of December, 1534, the first of these four ships arrived at the city of Seville. In her was the Captain Christoval de Mena, who brought 8000 *pesos* of gold and 950 *marcs* of silver. There was also on board a reverend clergyman, a native of Seville, named Juan de Losa, who brought 6000 *pesos* of gold and eighty *marcs* of silver. Beside these quantities, 38,946 *pesos* arrived in that ship.

In the year 1534, on the 9th of January, the second ship arrived, named the *Santa Maria de Campo*, with the Captain Hernando Pizarro on board, brother of Francisco Pizarro, the Governor and Captain-General of New Castille. In this ship there came, for his Majesty, 153,000 *pesos* of gold and 5048 *marcs* of silver. Besides this, several passengers and private persons brought 310,000 *pesos* of gold and 13,500 *marcs* of silver. This treasure came in bars and planks, and in pieces of gold and silver enclosed in large boxes.

In addition to all this, the ship brought, for his Majesty, thirty-eight vases of gold and forty-eight of silver, among which there was an eagle of silver. In its body were fitted two vases and two large pots, one of gold and the other of silver, each of which was capable of containing a cow cut into pieces. There were also two sacks of gold, each capable of holding two *fanegas* of wheat ; an idol of gold, the size of a child four years old; and two small drums. The other vases were of gold and silver, each one capable of holding two *arrobas* and more. In the same ship passengers brought home forty-four vases of silver and four of gold.

This treasure was landed on the mole and conveyed to

the *Casa de Contratacion*, the vases being carried, and the rest in twenty-six boxes, a pair of bullocks drawing a cart containing two boxes.

On the 3rd of July in the same year, three other ships arrived. The master of one was Francisco Rodriguez, and of the other Francisco Pabon. They brought, for passengers and private persons, 146,518 *pesos* of gold and 30,509 *marcs* of silver.

Without counting the above vases and pieces of gold and silver, the total amount of gold brought by these four ships was 708,580 *pesos*, a *peso* of gold being equal to a *castellano*. Each *peso* is commonly valued at 450 *maravedis*; so that, taking all the gold, except vases and other pieces, that was registered in these four ships, it would be worth 318,860,000 *maravedis*.

The silver was 49,008 *marcs*. Each *marc* is equal to eight ounces, which, counted at 2210 *maravedis*, makes the total value of the silver 108,307,680 *maravedis*.

One of the last two ships that arrived, in which Francisco Rodriguez was master, belonged to Francisco de Xeres, a native of the town of Seville, who wrote this narrative by order of the Governor Francisco Pizarro, being in the province of New Castille, in the city of Caxamalca, as Secretary to the Governor.

PRAISE TO GOD.

LETTER FROM HERNANDO PIZARRO

ROYAL AUDIENCE OF SANTO DOMINGO.

*To the Magnificent Lords, the Judges of the Royal Audience
of His Majesty who reside in the city of Santo Domingo.*

MAGNIFICENT LORDS,—I arrived in this port of Yaguana on
my way to Spain, by order of the Governor Francisco
Pizarro, to inform his Majesty of what has happened in that
government of Peru, to give an account of the country, and
of its present condition ; and, as I believe that those who
come to this city give your worships inconsistent accounts,
it has seemed well to me to write a summary of what has
taken place, that you may be informed of the truth, from
the time that Ysasaga came from that land, by whom your
worships will have been apprised of what had taken place
up to the time of his departure.

The Governor, in the name of his Majesty, founded a town
near the sea coast, which was called San Miguel. It is
twenty-five leagues from that point of Tumbez. Having
left citizens there, and assigned the Indians in the district
to them, he set out with sixty horse and ninety foot, in search
of the town of Caxamalca, at which place he was informed
that Atabaliva then was, the son of old Cuzco,[1] and brother
of him who is now Lord of that land.[2] Between the two

[1] Ynca Huayna Ccapac.
[2] The puppet set up by Francisco Pizarro, when he murdered Atahuallpa, and who died two months afterwards.

I

brothers[3] there had been a very fierce war, and this Atabaliva had conquered the land as far as he then was, which,
from the point whence he started, was a hundred and fifty
leagues. After seven or eight marches, a Captain of Atabaliva came to the Governor, and said that his Lord had
heard of his arrival and rejoiced greatly at it, having a strong
desire to see the Christians; and when he had been two
days with the Governor he said that he wished to go forward and tell the news to his Lord, and that another would
soon be on the road with a present, as a token of peace.
The Governor continued his march until he came to a town
called *La Ramada*.[4] Up to that point all the land was flat,
while all beyond was very rugged, and obstructed by very
difficult passes. When he saw that the messenger from
Atabaliva did not return, he wished to obtain intelligence
from some Indians who had come from Caxamalca; so they
were tortured,[5] and they then said that they had heard that
Atabaliva was waiting for the Governor in the mountains to
give him battle. The Governor then ordered the troops to advance, leaving the rear guard in the plain. The rest ascended,
and the road was so bad that, in truth, if they had been
waiting for us, either in this pass or in another that we came
to on the road to Caxamalca, they could very easily have
stopped us; for, even by exerting all our skill, we could
not have taken the horses by the roads; and neither horse
nor foot can cross those mountains except by the roads.
The distance across them to Caxamalca is twenty leagues.

When we were half-way, messengers arrived from Atabaliva, and brought provisions to the Governor. They said

---

[3] Ynca Huascar and Atahuallpa.

[4] A hut covered with the branches of trees. Apparently a name given
by the Spaniards to the place at which they halted, at the foot of the
mountains.

[5] This was the regular custom of Hernando Pizarro, to torture the
Indians before asking them questions. The consequence was, that he
was told lies, and as in this instance, as will be seen further on.

that Atabaliva was waiting for him at Caxamalca, wishing to be his friend; and that he wished the Governor to know that his captains, whom he has sent to the war of Cuzco, had taken his brother prisoner, that they would reach Caxamalca within two days, and that all the territory of his father now belonged to him. The Governor sent back to say that he rejoiced greatly at this news, and that if there was any Lord who refused to submit, he would give assistance and subjugate him. Two days afterwards the Governor came in sight of Caxamalca, and he met Indians with food. He put the troops in order, and marched to the town. Atabaliva was not there, but was encamped on the plain, at a distance of a league, with all his people in tents. When the Governor saw that Atabaliva did not come, he sent a Captain, with fifteen horsemen, to speak to Atabaliva, saying that he would not assign quarters to the Christians until he knew where it was the pleasure of Atabaliva that they should lodge, and he desired him to come that they might be friends. Just then I went to speak to the Governor, touching the orders in case the Indians made a night attack. He told me that he had sent men to seek an interview with Atabaliva. I told him that, out of the sixty cavalry we had, there might be some men who were not dexterous on horseback, and some unsound horses, and that it seemed a mistake to pick out fifteen of the best; for, if Atabaliva should attack them, their numbers were insufficient for defence, and any reverse might lead to a great disaster. He, therefore, ordered me to follow with other twenty horsemen, and to act according to circumstances.

When I arrived I found the other horsemen near the camp of Atabaliva, and that their officer had gone to speak with him. I left my men there also, and advanced with two horsemen to the lodging of Atabaliva, and the Captain announced my approach and who I was. I then told Atabaliva that the Governor had sent me to visit him, and to ask

him to come that they might be friends. He replied that a
Cacique of the town of San Miguel had sent to tell him
that we were bad people and not good for war, and that he
himself had killed some of us, both men and horses. I answered that those people of San Miguel were like women,
and that one horse was enough for the whole of them; that,
when he saw us fight, he would know what we were like;
that the Governor had a great regard for him; that if he
had any enemy he had only to say so, and that the Governor
would send to conquer him. He said that, four marches
from that spot, there were some very rebellious Indians who
would not submit to him, and that the Christians might go
there to help his troops. I said that the Governor would
send ten horsemen, who would suffice for the whole country,
and that his Indians were unnecessary, except to search for
those who concealed themselves. He smiled like a man
who did not think so much of us. The Captain told me
that, until I came, he had not been able to get him to speak,
but that one of his chiefs had answered for him, while he
always kept his head down. He was seated in all the
majesty of command, surrounded by all his women, and
with many chiefs near him. Before coming to his presence
there was another group of chiefs, each standing according
to his rank. At sunset I said that I wished to go, and
asked him to tell me what to say to the Governor. He replied that he would come to see him on the following morning, that he would lodge in three great chambers in the
courtyard, and that the centre one should be set apart for
himself.

That night a good look-out was kept. In the morning
he sent messengers to put off his visit until the afternoon;
and these messengers, in conversing with some Indian girls
in the service of the Christians, who were their relations,
told them to run away because Atabaliva was coming that
afternoon to attack the Christians and kill them. Among

the messengers there came that Captain who had already
met the Governor on the road. He told the Governor that
his Lord Atabaliva said that, as the Christians had come
armed to his camp, he also would come armed. The Governor replied that he might come as he liked. Atabaliva
set out from his camp at noon, and when he came to a place
which was about half a quarter of a league from Caxamalca,
he stopped until late in the afternoon. There he pitched
his tents, and formed his men in three divisions. The whole
road was full of men, and they had not yet left off marching
out of the camp. The Governor had ordered his troops to
be distributed in the three halls (*galpones*)[6] which were in
the open courtyard, in form of a triangle ; and he ordered
them to be mounted and armed until the intentions of Atabaliva were known. Having pitched his tents, Atabaliva
sent a messenger to the Governor to say that, as it was now
late, he wished to sleep where he was, and that he would
come in the morning. The Governor sent back to beg
him to come at once, because he was waiting for supper,
and that he should not sup until Atabaliva should come.
The messengers came back to ask the Governor to send a
Christian to Atabaliva, that he intended to come at once,
and that he would come unarmed. The Governor sent a
Christian,[7] and presently Atabaliva moved, leaving the armed
men behind him. He took with him about five or six
thousand Indians without arms, except that, under their
shirts, they had small darts and slings with stones.

[6] The word *galpon* is not Spanish. Garcilasso says that it belonged
to the language of the Windward Islands, and that the Spaniards adopted
it. The word means a large hall or court. The Yncas had such halls
attached to their palaces, which were so large that festivals were held in
them, when the weather was rainy. Such vast halls may still be seen
among the ruins of Hervay and Pachacamac. In Cuzco they have been
converted into modern houses. The villages of slaves in modern *haci-
endas* on the Peruvian coast, which are enclosed by high walls, are called
galpones.

[7] Xeres says that he refused to send the Christian. See p. 50.

He came in a litter, and before him went three or four hundred Indians in liveries,[8] cleaning the straws from the road and singing. Then came Atabaliva in the midst of his chiefs and principal men, the greatest among them being also borne on men's shoulders. When they entered the open space, twelve or fifteen Indians went up to the little fortress that was there and occupied it, taking possession with a banner fixed on a lance. When Atabaliva had advanced to the centre of the open space, he stopped, and a Dominican Friar, who was with the Governor, came forward to tell him, on the part of the Governor, that he waited for him in his lodging, and that he was sent to speak with him. The Friar then told Atabaliva that he was a Priest, and that he was sent there to teach the things of the Faith, if they should desire to be Christians. He showed Atabaliva a book which he carried in his hands, and told him that that book contained the things of God. Atabaliva asked for the book, and threw it on the ground, saying :—" I will not leave this place until you have restored all that you have taken in my land. I know well who you are, and what you have come for." Then he rose up in his litter, and addressed his men, and there were murmurs among them and calls to those who were armed. The Friar went to the Governor and reported what was being done, and that no time was to be lost. The Governor sent to me ; and I had arranged with the Captain of the artillery that, when a sign was given, he should discharge his pieces, and that, on hearing the reports, all the troops should come forth at once. This was done, and as the Indians were unarmed, they were defeated without danger to any Christian. Those who carried the litter, and the chiefs who surrounded Atabaliva, were all killed, falling round him. The Governor came out and seized Atabaliva, and, in protecting him, he received a knife-

[8] In liveries of different colours, like a chess-board, Xeres tells us. See p. 53.

cut from a Christian in the hand. The troops continued the
pursuit as far as the place where the armed Indians were
stationed, who made no resistance whatever, because it was
now night. All were brought into the town, where the
Governor was quartered.

Next morning the Governor ordered us to go to the camp
of Atabaliva, where we found forty thousand *castellanos* and
four or five thousand *marcos* of silver. The camp was as
full of people as if none were wanting. All the people were
assembled, and the Governor desired them to go to their
homes, and told them that he had not come to do them
harm, that what he had done was by reason of the pride of
Atabaliva, and that he himself ordered it. On asking Atabaliva why he had thrown away the book and shown so
much pride, he answered that his captain, who had been
sent to speak with the Governor, had told him that the
Christians were not warriors, that the horses were unsaddled
at night, and that with two hundred Indians he could defeat
them all. He added that this captain and the chief of San
Miguel had deceived him. The Governor then inquired
concerning his brother the Cuzco,[9] and he answered that he
would arrive next day, that he was being brought as a
prisoner, and that his captain remained with the troops in
the town of Cuzco. It afterwards turned out that in all this
he had spoken the truth, except that he had sent orders for
his brother to be killed, lest the Governor should restore
him to his lordship. The Governor said that he had not
come to make war on the Indians, but that our Lord the
Emperor, who was Lord of the whole world, had ordered
him to come that he might see the land, and let Atabaliva
know the things of our Faith, in case he should wish to become a Christian. The Governor also told him that that
land, and all other lands, belonged to the Emperor, and
that he must acknowledge him as his Lord. He replied that

[9] Ynca Huascar.

he was content, and, observing that the Christians had collected some gold, Atabaliva said to the Governor that they need not take such care of it, as if there was so little ; for that he could give them ten thousand plates,[1] and that he could fill the room in which he was up to a white line, which was the height of a man and a half from the floor. The room was seventeen or eighteen feet wide, and thirty-five feet long. He said that he could do this in two months.

Two months passed away, and the gold did not arrive, but the Governor received tidings that every day parties of men were advancing against him. In order both to ascertain the truth of these reports, and to hurry the arrival of the gold, the Governor ordered me to set out with twenty horsemen and ten or twelve foot soldiers for a place called Guamachuco, which is twenty leagues from Caxamalca. This was the place where it was reported that armed men were collecting together. I advanced to that town, and found a quantity of gold and silver, which I sent thence to Caxamalca. Some Indians, who were tortured,[2] told us that the captains and armed men were at a place six leagues from Guamachuco ; and, though I had no instructions from the Governor to advance beyond that point, I resolved to push forward with fourteen horsemen and nine foot soldiers, in order that the Indians might not take heart at the notion that we had retreated. The rest of my party were sent to guard the gold, because their horses were lame. Next morning I arrived at that town, and did not find any armed men there, and it turned out that the Indians had told lies; perhaps to frighten us and induce us to return.

At this village I received permission from the Governor to go to a mosque of which we had intelligence, which was

---

[1] *Tejuelos*, square pieces of metal, on which the points of gates or large doors turn. Quoits are also called *tejuelos*.

[2] Here the ruffian is at his torturing tricks again ; and is again only told lies for his pains.

a hundred leagues away on the sea-coast, in a town called
Pachacamá. It took us twenty-two days to reach it. The
road over the mountains is a thing worth seeing, because,
though the ground is so rugged, such beautiful roads could
not in truth be found throughout Christendom. The greater
part of them is paved. There is a bridge of stone or wood
over every stream. We found bridges of network over a
very large and powerful river, which we crossed twice,
which was a marvellous thing to see. The horses crossed
over by them. At each passage they have two bridges, the
one by which the common people go over, and the other for
the lords of the land and their captains. The approaches
are always kept closed, with Indians to guard them. These
Indians exact transit dues from all passengers. The chiefs
and people of the mountains are more intelligent than those
of the coast. The country is populous. There are mines in
many parts of it. It is a cold climate, it snows, and there
is much rain. There are no swamps. Fuel is scarce. Atabaliva has placed governors in all the principal towns, and
his predecessors had also appointed governors. In all these
towns there were houses of imprisoned women, with guards
at the doors, and these women preserve their virginity. If
any Indian has any connection with them his punishment is
death. Of these houses, some are for the worship of the
Sun, others for that of old Cuzco,[3] the father of Atabaliva.
Their sacrifices consist of sheep and *chicha*,[4] which they
pour out on the ground. They have another house of
women in each of the principal towns, also guarded. These
women are assembled by the chiefs of the neighbouring
districts, and when the lord of the land passes by they select
the best to present to him, and when they are taken others
are chosen to fill up their places. These women also have
the duty of making *chicha* for the soldiers when they pass

[3] The Ynca Huayna Ccapac.
[4] Fermented liquor from maize.

that way.   They took Indian girls out of these houses and
presented them to us.   All the surrounding chiefs come to
these towns on the roads to perform service when the army
passes.   They have stores of fuel and maize, and of all other
necessaries.   They count by certain knots on cords, and so
record what each chief has brought.   When they had to
bring us loads of fuel, maize, chicha, or meat, they took off
knots or made knots on some other part ; so that those who
have charge of the stores keep an exact account.   In all
these towns they received us with great festivities, dancing
and rejoicing.

When we arrived on the plains of the sea coast we met
with a people who were less civilised, but the country was
populous.   They also have houses of women, and all the
other arrangements as in the towns of the mountains.   They
never wished to speak to us of the mosque, for there was an
order that all who should speak to us of it should be put to
death.   But as we had intelligence that it was on the coast,
we followed the high road until we came to it.   The road is
very wide, with an earthen wall on either side, and houses
for resting at intervals, which were prepared to receive the
Cuzco when he travelled that way.   There are very large
villages, the houses of the Indians being built of canes ; and
those of the chiefs are of earth with roofs of branches of
trees ; for in that land it never rains.   From the city of San
Miguel to this mosque the distance is one hundred and
sixty or one hundred and eighty leagues, the road passing
near the sea shore through a very populous country.   The
road, with a wall on each side, traverses the whole of this
country ; and, neither in that part nor in the part further
on, of which we had notice for two hundred leagues, does it
ever rain.   They live by irrigation, for the rainfall is so
great in the mountains that many rivers flow from them, so
that throughout the land there is not three leagues without
a river.   The distance from the sea to the mountains is in

some parts ten leagues, in others twelve. It is not cold. Throughout the whole of this coast land, and beyond it, tribute is not paid to Cuzco, but to the mosque. The bishop of it was in Caxamalca with the Governor. He had ordered another room of gold, such as Atabaliva had ordered, and the Governor ordered me to go on this business, and to hurry those who were collecting it. When I arrived at the mosque, I asked for the gold, and they denied it to me, saying that they had none. I made some search, but could not find it. The neighbouring chiefs came to see me, and brought presents, and in the mosque there was found some gold dust, which was left behind when the rest was concealed. Altogether I collected 85,000 *castellanos* and 3000 *marcos* of silver.

This town of the mosque is very large, and contains grand edifices and courts. Outside, there is another great space surrounded by a wall, with a door opening on the mosque. In this space there are the houses of the women, who, they say, are the women of the devil. Here, also, are the storerooms, where the stores of gold are kept. There is no one in the place where these women are kept. Their sacrifices are the same as those to the Sun, which I have already described. Before entering the first court of the mosque, a man must fast for twenty days; before ascending to the court above, he must fast for a year. In this upper court the bishop used to be. When messengers of the chiefs, who had fasted for a year, went up to pray to God that he would give them a good harvest, they found the bishop seated, with his head covered. There are other Indians whom they call pages of the Sun. When these messengers of the chief delivered their messages to the bishop, the pages of the devil went into a chamber, where they said that he speaks to them; and that devil said that he was enraged with the chiefs, with the sacrifices they had to offer, and with the presents they wished to bring. I believe that they do not speak with the devil, but that these his servants deceive the chiefs. For I took pains to investigate the matter, and an old page, who was one of the chief and most confidential servants of their god, told a chief, who repeated it to me, that the devil said they were not to fear the horses, as they could do no harm. I caused the page to be tortured, and he was so stubborn in his evil creed, that I could never gather anything from him, but that they really held their devil to be a god. This mosque is so feared by all the Indians, that they believe that if any of those servants of the devil asked them for anything and they refused it, they would presently die. It would seem that the Indians do not worship this devil from any feelings of devotion, but from fear. For the chiefs told me that, up to that time, they had served that mosque because they feared it; but that now they had no fear but of us, and that, therefore, they wished to serve us. The cave in which the devil was placed was very dark, so that one could not enter it without a light, and within it was very dirty. I made all the Caciques, who came to see me, enter the place that they might lose their fear; and, for want of a preacher, I made my sermon, explaining to them the errors in which they lived.

In this town I learnt that the principal Captain of Atabaliva[5] was at a distance of twenty leagues from us, in a town called Jauja. I sent to tell him to come and see me, and he replied that I should take the road to Caxamalca, and that he would take another road and meet me. The Governor, on hearing that the Captain was for peace and that he was ready to come with me, wrote to me to tell me to return; and he sent three Christians to Cuzco, which is fifty leagues beyond Jauja, to take possession and to see the country. I returned by the road of Caxamalca, and by another road, where the Captain of Atabaliva was to join me. But he had not started; and I learnt from certain

[5] This was Chalcuchima.

chiefs that he had not moved, and that he had taken me in. So I went back to the place where he was, and the road was very rugged, and so obstructed with snow, that it cost us much labour to get there. Having reached the royal road, and come to a place called Bombon, I met a Captain of Atabaliva with five thousand armed Indians whom Atabaliva had sent on pretence of conquering a rebel chief; but, as it afterwards appeared, they were assembled to kill the Christians. Here we found 500,000 *pesos* of gold that they were taking to Caxamalca. This Captain told me that the Captain-General remained in Jauja, that he knew of our approach, and was much afraid. I sent a messenger to him, to tell him to remain where he was, and to fear nothing. I also found a negro here, who had gone with the Christians to Cuzco, and he told me that these fears were feigned; for that the Captain-General[6] had many well-armed men with him, that he counted them by his knots in presence of the Christians, and that they numbered thirty-five thousand Indians. So we went to Jauja, and, when we were half a league from the town, and found that the Captain did not come out to receive us, a chief of Atabaliva, whom I had with me and whom I had treated well, advised me to advance in order of battle, because he believed that the Captain intended to fight. We went up a small hill overlooking Jauja, and saw a large black mass in the *plaza*, which appeared to be something that had been burnt. I asked what it was, and they told me that it was a crowd of Indians. The *plaza* is large, and has a length of a quarter of a league. As no one came to receive us on reaching the town, our people advanced in the expectation of having to fight the Indians. But, at the entrance of the *square*, some principal men came out to meet us with offers of peace, and told us that the Captain was not there, as he had gone to reduce certain chiefs to submission. It would seem that he had gone out

[6] Chalcuchima.

of fear with some of his troops, and had crossed a river
near the town by a bridge of network. I sent to tell him
to come to me peaceably, or else the Christians would destroy him. Next morning the people came who were in
the square. They were Indian servants, and it is true that
they numbered over a hundred thousand souls. We remained
here five days, and during all that time they did nothing
but dance and sing, and hold great drinking feasts. The
Captain did not wish to come with me, but when he saw
that I was determined to make him, he came of his own
accord. I left the chief who came with me as Captain there.
This town of Jauja is very fine and picturesque, with very
good level approaches, and it has an excellent river bank.
In all my travels I did not see a better site for a Christian
settlement, and I believe that the Governor intends to form
one there, though some think that it would be more convenient to select a position near the sea, and are, therefore,
of an opposite opinion. All the country, from Jauja to
Caxamalca, by the road we returned, is like that of which
I have already given a description.

After returning to Caxamalca, and reporting my proceedings to the Governor, he ordered me to go to Spain,
and to give an account to his Majesty of this and other
things which appertain to his service. I took, from the
heap of gold, 100,000 *castellanos* for his Majesty, being the
amount of his fifth. The day after I left Caxamalca, the
Christians, who had gone to Cuzco, returned, and brought
1,500,000 of gold. After I arrived at Panama, another
ship came in, with some knights. They say that a distribution of the gold was made ; and that the share of his
Majesty, besides the 100,000 *pesos* and the 5000 *marcos* of
silver that I bring, was another 165,000 *castellanos*, and
7000 or 8000 *marcos* of silver ; while to all those of us who
had gone, a further share of gold was sent.

After my departure, according to what the Governor

writes to me, it became known that Atabaliva had assembled troops to make war on the Christians, and justice was done upon him. The Governor made his brother, who was his enemy, lord in his place. Molina comes to this city, and from him your worships may learn anything else that you may desire to know. The shares of the troops were, to the horsemen 9000 *castellanos*, to the Governor 6000, to me 3000. The Governor has derived no other profit from that land, nor has there been deceit or fraud in the account. I say this to your worships, because if any other statement is made, this is the truth. May our Lord long guard and prosper the magnificent persons of your worships.

Done in this city, November 1533. At the service of your worships.

HERNANDO PIZARRO.

REPORT

ON THE

DISTRIBUTION OF THE RANSOM

OF

ATAHUALLPA.

BY

PEDRO SANCHO (Notary).

REPORT ON THE DISTRIBUTION

OF THE

RANSOM OF ATAHUALLPA,

CERTIFIED BY THE

NOTARY PEDRO SANCHO.

In the town of Caxamalca, of these kingdoms of New Castille, on the 17th day of the month of June, in the year of
the birth of our Lord Jesus Christ, 1533, the very magnificent Lord and Commander Francisco Pizarro, Adelantado,
Lieutenant, Captain-General, and Governor for his Majesty
in the said kingdoms, in the presence of me, Pedro Sancho,
Lieutenant of the General Secretary, on the part of the
Lord Pedro Samano, declares : that, on the occasion of the
imprisonment and defeat of the chief Atahuallpa and of his
troops in this town, some gold was collected, and that afterwards the said chief promised to the Christian Spaniards
that they should find a certain quantity of gold in his prison,
which quantity should, he declared, be a room full, namely,
10,000 *tejuelos*, and much silver which he possessed and
promised ; and which his captains, in his name, had taken
in the war and capture of Cuzco, and in the conquest of
those lands, by many ways which are more fully declared in
the act which was attested before a notary ; and which the
said chief has given, brought, and ordered to be given
and brought : of which a division and distribution has been
made, as well of the gold as the silver, and of the pearls and
emeralds which have been given, and of their value, among
the persons who were present at the capture of the said
chief, and who acquired and took the said gold and silver,

and to whom the said chief promised, gave, and delivered it; so that each person might have, hold, and possess that which belonged to him; in order that his Lordship might without delay settle the matter, and leave this town to go and people and reduce the land beyond, and for many other reasons which are not herein stated; for which object the said Lord Governor declared that his Majesty, in his provisions and royal orders, in which he granted the government of these kingdoms, commanded that all the fruits and other things that in these lands might be found and acquired, should be given and distributed among the conquerors who should acquire them, in the way that seemed best to him, and according as each person should deserve by reason of his rank and services; and considering the above said commands, and other things that ought to be considered in making the distribution, and that each man might have his share of what the chief had given, as his Majesty had commanded, he has determined to name and select before me, the said notary, the quantity of silver which each person shall have and take, according as, in his conscience, God our Lord shall give him understanding; and, for the better performance, he seeks the aid of God our Lord, and invokes his divine assistance.

Then the said Lord Governor, considering what is said and declared in the deed, having God before his eyes, assigned to each person the *marcos* of silver that he had earned and deserved, out of what the said chief had given, and in this manner it was arranged.

On the 18th of June of the same year of 1533, the said Governor approved another deed, by which the gold was to be melted and distributed; and the gold was melted and distributed in this manner. I distinguish the gold and silver that each one received in the following columns; that the list of persons may only be given once.

	Marcos of silver.	Pesos of gold.
To the Church	90...	2220
To the Lord Governor, for his persons, his interpreters, and horse	2350...	57220
To Hernando Pizarro	1267...	31080
To Hernando de Soto	724...	17740
To Father Juan de Sosa, Chaplain to the army	310...	7770
To Juan Pizarro	407...	11100
To PEDRO DE CANDIA[1]	407...	9909
To Gonzalo Pizarro	384...	9909
To Juan Córtes	362...	9430
To Sebastian de Benalcazar[2]	407...	9909
To Cristobal Mena, or Medina	366...	8380
To Luis Hernandez Bueno	384...	9435
To Juan de Salazar	362...	9435
To Miguel Estete[3]	362...	8980
To Francisco de Jerez	362...	8880
More to the said Jerez and Pedro Sancho for writing	94...	2220
To Gonzalo de Pineda[4]	384...	9909
To ALONZO BRICEÑO[5]	362...	8380
To Alonzo de Medina	362...	8480
To Juan Pizarro de Orellana[6]	362...	8980
To Luis Marca	362...	8880

[1] One of the thirteen. See Note at p. 8.

[2] For some account of the career of Benalcazar see my translations of *Pascual de Andagoya;* and of *Cieza de Leon.* Note at p. 110.

[3] See Note at p. 74.

[4] Killed by Indians who captured him, in the war between Gonzalo Pizarro and the Viceroy Blasco Nunez. *G. de la Vega,* ii, lib. iv, p. 24.

[5] One of the thirteen. See Note at p. 8.

[6] Went with Hernando Pizarro to Pachacamac. *G. de la Vega,* ii, lib. i, cap. 29.

To Geronimo de Aliaga[7]	. . .	339...8880
To Gonzalo Perez	. . .	362...8880
To Pedro de Barrientos	. . .	362...8880
To Rodrigo Nuñez[8]	. . .	362...8880
To Pedro Anades	. . .	362...8880
To Francisco Maraver	. . .	362...7770
To Diego Maldonado[9]	. . .	362...7770
To Ramiro or FRANCISCO DE CHAVES[1]	. . .	362...8880
To Diego Ojuelos	. . .	362..8880
To Gines de Carranca	. . .	362...8880
To Juan de Quincoces	. . .	362...8880
To Alonzo de Morales	. . .	362...8880
To Lope Velez .	. . .	362...8880
To Juan de Barbaian[2]	. . .	362...8880
To Pedro de Aguirre	. . .	362...8880
To Pedro de Leon	. . .	362...8880
To Diego Mejia	. . .	362...8880
To Martin Alonzo	. . .	362...8880
To Juan de Rosas	. . .	362...8880
To Pedro Cataño	. . .	362...8880

[7] He was appointed Governor of Lima by Vaca de Castro, and distinguished himself in the battle of Chupas against the younger Almagro. *G. de la Vega*, II, lib. ii, caps. 12 and 18.

[8] He was put to death on suspicion, by Gonzalo Pizarro, at Lima. *G. de la Vega*, II, lib. iv, cap. 20.

[9] A very conspicuous personage in the future civil wars. He took a part in them all, down to the insurrection of Giron. He was surnamed "the rich", and became a citizen of Cuzco, where he died in 1562. Frequent mention of him will be found in *Garcilasso*.

[1] See Note at p. 104.

[2] It should be Juan de Barbaran. He was a native of Truxillo, and was a servant of the Conqueror. When Pizarro was murdered no man dared to bury the body, for fear of the assassins, until the faithful Barbaran and his wife performed the office in the best way they could, dressing the body in the mantle of Santiago. Barbaran afterwards fought bravely against the younger Almagro at the battle of Chupas. *G. de la Vega*, II, lib. iii, cap. 7.

To Pedro Ortiz[3]	.	.	. 362...8880
To Juan Morquejo	.	.	. 362...8880
To Hernando de Toro	.	.	. 316...8880
To Diego de Aguero[4]	.	.	. 362...8880
To Alonzo Perez	.	.	. 362...8880
To Hernando Beltran	.	.	. 362...8880
To Pedro de Barrera	.	.	. 362...8880
To Francisco de Baena	.	.	. 362...8880
To Francisco Lopez	.	.	. 371...8880
To Sebastian de Torres	.	.	. 362...8880
To Juan Ruiz	.	.	. 339...8880
To FRANCISCO DE FUENTES[5]		.	. 362...8880
To Gonzalo del Castillo	.	.	. 362...8880
To Nicolas de Azpitia	.	.	. 339...8880
To Diego de Molina	.	.	. 316...7770
To Alonzo Peto	.	.	. 316...7770
To Miguel Ruiz	.	.	. 362...8880
To Juan de Salinas[6] (blacksmith)	.	.	. 362...8880
To Juan Loz	.	.	. 248...6110
To Cristobal Gallego (no gold)	.	.	. 316... —
To Rodrigo de Cantillana (no gold)		.	. 248... —
To Gabriel Telor (no gold)	.	.	. 294... —
To Hernan Sanchez[7]	.	.	. 262...8880
To Pedro Sa Paramo	.	.	. 271...6115

[3] Pedro Ortiz de Orue became a citizen of Cuzco, and married a sister of the Ynca Sayri Tupac. See Note at p. 253 of vol. ii of my translation of *Garcilasso de la Vega*, Part I.

[4] When the Indians rose against the Spaniards, under Ynca Manco, Diego de Aguero received timely notice from the Indian servants on his estate, and escaped into Lima. After the murder of Pizarro, he fled from the Almagro faction, and joined Vaca de Castro at Truxillo. He also persuaded the people of Lima to receive the unpopular Viceroy Blasco Nuñez. He seems to have been a loyal, peaceable man.

[5] One of the twelve who protested against the murder of Atahuallpa. See Note at p. 103.

[6] *G. de la Vega*, II, lib. viii, cap. 13.

[7] Hernan Sanchez de Vargas was abandoned on the desert shore of

Infantry.

To Juan de Porras	.	.	. 181...4540
To Gregorio Sotelo	.	.	. 181...4540
To Pedro Sancho	.	.	. 181...4540
To Garcia de Paredes	.	.	. 181...4540
To Juan de Baldivieso	.	.	. 181...4540
To Gonzalo Maldonado	.	.	. 181...4540
To Pedro Navarro	،	.	. 181...4540
To Juan Ronquillo	.	.	. 181...4540
To Antonio de Bergara	.	.	. 181...4540
To Alonzo de la Carrera	.	.	. 181...4540
To Alonzo Romero	.	.	. 181...4540
To Melchor Berdugo[8]	.	.	. 135...3330
To Martin Bueno[9]	.	.	. 135...4440
To Juan Perez Tudela	.	.	. 181...4440
To Inigo Taburco	.	.	. 181...4440

the Napo, by Orellana, when he descended the Amazon. See my *Valley of the Amazons*, p. 12.

[8] Melchior Verdugo was a native of Avila. He received a large grant in the valley of Caxamarca. He distinguished himself in the battle of Chupas against Almagro the younger. He was a friend of the Viceroy Blasco Nuñez de Vela; and when Gonzalo Pizarro rebelled and declared himself Governor of Peru, his Lieutenant Carbajal seized Verdugo at Lima, and put him in prison. He was afterwards allowed to go to his own house in Truxillo. There he played the party of Gonzalo Pizarro an extraordinary trick. A ship was at anchor in the port, and he invited the captain and pilot to his house, and locked them up. He then looked out of his window and saw the Alcalde and others. He called to them, begging them to come up and witness a deed, as he had a pain in his feet and could not go down. Up they came, suspecting nothing, and were locked up also. He did the same to about twenty of the leading men of Gonzalo's party, and then seized the ship, sailing in her to Nicaragua, with a few followers; and a quantity of gold and silver, which he had extorted from his captives. He was chased by some vessels of Gonzalo, and his ship was seized, after he had landed. After staying some time in Nicaragua and at Carthagena, he went to Spain and received the habit of Santiago. He returned to Peru in 1563.

[9] One of the three soldiers who were sent to Cuzco by Pizarro. See p. 72. (Note.)

To Nuño Gonzalo (*no gold*) . . 111... —
To Juan de Herrera . . . 158...3385
To Francisco Davalos . . . 181...4440
To Hernando de Aldana . . . 181...4440
To Martin de Marquina . . . 135...3330
To Antonio de Herrera . . . 136...3330
To Sandoval (*Chistian name not given*) . 135...3330
To Miguel Estete[1] de Santiago . . 135...3330
To Juan Bonallo . . . 181...4440
To Pedro Moguer[2] . . . 181...4440
To Francisco Perez . . . 158...3880
To Melchor Palomino . . . 158...3330
To Pedro de Alconchel . . . 135...4440
To Juan de Segovia . . . 181...3330
To Crisostomo de Ontiveros . . 135...3330
To Hernan Muñoz . . . 135...3330
To Alonso de Mesa[3] . . . 135...3330
To Juan Perez de Oma . . . 135...3885
To DIEGO DE TRUXILLO[4] . . . 158...3330

[1] See Note at p. 74.
[2] One of the three soldiers who were sent to Cuzco by Pizarro. See p. 72. (Note.)
[3] Alonzo de Mesa became a citizen of Cuzco, and had a house next door to that of Garcilasso de la Vega (ii, p. 254). He had a very pretty girl living in his house, and when young Altamirano was riding a race, he kept looking back at her in Mesa's balcony, until he fell off. In the rebellion of Giron in 1550, Mesa fled from Cuzco, and the licentiate Alvarado, Giron's lieutenant, discovered and dug up sixty bars of silver, worth three hundred ducats each, in the fugitive's back garden. Young Garcilasso saw the robbers at work, from a window of his father's house. Mesa's son, also named Alonzo, and probably a half-caste, was employed by the Ynca family as their advocate in Spain, in 1603.
[4] According to Garcilasso de la Vega, this Diego de Truxillo was one of the men who stood by Pizarro on the island of Gallo. See Note at p. 8. He had large estates near Cuzco, and was imprisoned there by Almagro, when he came back from Chile and seized the Pizarros and their adherents. He afterwards distinguished himself in the battle of Chupas against the younger Almagro. In the rebellion of Giron he remained

To Palomino (*cooper*) . . . 181...4440
To Alonzo Jimenez . . . 181...4440
To Pedro de Torres . . . 135...3330
To Alonzo de Toro[5] . . . 135...3330
To Diego Lopez[6] . . . 135...3330
To Francisco Gallegosa . . . 135...3330
To Bonilla . . . . 181...4440
To Francisco de Almendras[7] . . 181...4440
To Escalante . . . . 181...3330

loyal, and joined the Marshal Alvarado. The historian Garcilasso knew Diego de Truxillo at Cuzco, and he was still living there in 1560.

[5] When the Ynca Manco besieged Cuzco, Gonzalo Pizarro sallied out as far as the lake of Chinchero, two leagues to the north, where he was attacked by a large army of Indians. He would have been overpowered, had not his brother Hernando Pizarro and Alonzo de Toro come out to the rescue. When Gonzalo Pizarro rebelled against the Viceroy Blasco Nuñez, he appointed Alonzo de Toro to be his Master of the Camp at Cuzco, but he fell ill on the road to Lima, and Carbajal took his place. Toro returned to Cuzco, where he heard that Diego Centeno had risen against Gonzalo Pizarro. He then collected some troops, and pursued Centeno as far as La Plata (Chuquisaca) in the extreme south of Peru, returning to Cuzco. There appears to have been much jealousy between Toro and Carbajal. While Alonzo de Toro was Governor of Cuzco for Gonzalo Pizarro, he married a daughter of one Diego Gonzalez de Vargas. They all lived together. One day the father-in-law came home, and found his daughter and her husband quarrelling. Alonzo was proud and quick-tempered. Diego Gonzalez was an old man, more than sixty-five. Alonzo rushed at his father-in-law, calling him names. In self-defence the old man drew a dagger ; Alonzo rushed upon it, and received a mortal wound.

[6] Probably Diego Lopez de Zuñiga, who served under Centeno, at the battle of Huarina; and was afterwards named a Captain of Infantry by the Royal Audience, to serve against Giron.

[7] Francisco de Almendras settled in Charcas and became very rich. He was very kind to Diego Centeno, who came out to Peru very young, and treated him as his own son. Indeed, they were called father and son. Almendras became Governor of La Plata (Chuquisaca) for Gonzalo Pizarro ; where Centeno ungratefully put him to death, as a commencement of his insurrection on the side of loyalty, and against Gonzalo. But Zarate gives Almendras a very bad character. (*Hist. del Peru*, lib. v, cap. 21.)

To Andres Jimenez	. . .	181...3330
To Juan Jimenez	. . .	181...3330
To Garcia Martin	. . .	135...3330
To Alonzo Ruiz	. . .	·135...3330
To Lucas Martinez	. . .	135...3330
To Gomez Gonzalez	. . .	135...3330
To Alonzo de Albuquerque	. .	94...2220
To Francisco de Vargas .	. .	181...4440
To Diego Gavilan[8]	. .	181...3884
To Contreras (*dead*)	. .	133...2770
To Rodrigo de Herrera (*musketeer*) .	.	135...3330
To Martin de Florencia[9] .	. .	135...3330
To Anton de Oviedo	. .	135...3330
To Jorge Griego	. .	181...4440
To Pedro de San Millan[1]	. .	135...3330

[8] Diego Gavilan was a man of good family, but he was unlucky. He settled at Cuzco, and in 1550 he was still poor ; so Giron persuaded him to join in his rebellion, and to become a Captain of Horse in the insurgent army. When Giron fled from Pucara, Gavilan went over to the royal army, and obtained his pardon.

[9] He did not wish to join the rebellion of Gonzalo Pizarro, and was therefore hanged at Lima by cruel old Carbajal, together with Pedro del Barco.

[1] Pedro de San Millan became a partizan of Almagro, and he was one of the thirteen assassins who, led by Juan de Rada, ran across the square of Lima to murder Pizarro, on Sunday, the 26th of June, 1541. They ran with their drawn swords, shouting, "Death to the tyrant!" Rushing up the stairs of Pizarro's house, they were met by Francisco de Chaves, who tried to stop them. He received a sword-thrust, and a cut which nearly severed his head, and the body was hurled down the steps. Dr. Velasquez and the servants, hearing the noise, escaped out of the windows into a garden. Pizarro was defended by his half-brother, Francisco Martin de Alcantara, and by two young pages, Juan de Vargas, a son of Gomez de Tordoya, and Alonzo Escandon. They had no time to put on armour ; but Pizarro and his brother defended the door-way with great bravery, for a long time. At last Alcantara was slain, and one of the pages took his place. Then Juan de Rada seized one of the other assassins, named Narvaez, and hurled him against Pizarro, who received him on his dagger, and killed him. But, in the scuffle, the

To Pedro Catalan	. . .	93...3330
To Pedro Roman	. . .	93...2220
To Francisco de la Torre	. .	131...2775
To Francisco Gorducho .	.	135...3330
To Juan Perez de Gomora	. .	181...4440
To Diego de Narvaez .	.	113...2775
To Gabriel de Olivarez .	.	181...4440
To Juan Garcia de Santa Olalla	.	135...3330
To PEDRO DE MENDOZA[2] .	.	135...3330
To Juan Garcia (*musketeer*)	.	135...3330
To Juan Perez	. .	135...3330
To Francisco Martin[3] .	.	135...3330
To Bartolomé Sanchez (*sailor*)	.	135...3330
To Martin Pizarro .	.	135...3330
To Hernando de Montalvo	.	181...3330
To Pedro Pinelo .	.	135...3330
To Lazaro Sanchez .	.	94...3330
To Miguel Cornejo[4] .	.	135...3330

others rushed into the room. The two young pages fell fighting bravely, after having severely wounded four of the assassins. Pizarro was thus left alone. The murderers attacked him on all sides, and at last he was stabbed in the throat. He fell to the ground, made the sign of the Cross on the floor with his right hand, kissed it, and expired. Four of the assassins were killed, and four wounded. Of the others, Cristoval de Sosa's name occurs in this list, further on; Martin de Bilbao was hanged and quartered after the battle of Chupas; Juan de Rada died at Xauxa before the battle; Diego Mendez (a brother of Orgoñez) fled to the court of the Ynca Manco in the mountains of Vilcapampa, where he was killed, with some other Spaniards, because one of them murdered the Ynca; Martin Carrillo was killed in the battle of Chupas; Gomez Perez was the actual murderer of the Ynca Manco, and was killed with Mendez. The other two were obscure men, and their fate is unknown.

[2] One of the twelve who protested against the murder of Atahuallpa. See Note at p. 103.

[3] Francisco Martin de Alcantara, the uterine brother of Francisco Pizarro. He was killed by the assassins of Pizarro, while striving to defend him.

[4] Miguel Cornejo settled at Arequipa. When old Francisco de Carbajal (afterwards the famous Lieutenant of Gonzalo Pizarro) first came

To Francisco Gonzalez	.	. 94...3330
To Francisco Martinez	.	. 135...3330
To Çarate[5] (*no Christian name*)	.	. 182...4440
To Hernando de Loja	:	. 135...3330
To Juan de Niza	.	. 195...3330
To Francisco de Solar	.	. 94...3330
To Hernando de Jemendo	.	. 67...2220
To Juan Sanchez	.	. 94...1663
To Sancho de Villegas	.	. 135...3330
To Pedro de Velva (*no gold*)	.	. 94... —
To Juan Chico	.	. 135...3330
To Rodas (*tailor*)	.	. 94...2000
To Pedro Salinas de la Hoz	.	. 125...3330
To Anton Estevan Garcia	.	. 186...2220
To Juan Delgado Menzon	.	. 139...3220
To Pedro de Valencia	.	. 94...2220
To Alonzo Sanchez Talavera	.	. 94...2220
To Miguel Sanchez	.	. 135...3330
To Juan Garcia (*common crier*)	.	. 103...2775

to Peru, he was very poor. He arrived at Arequipa, with his wife Doña Catalina Leyton and two servants, on his way to Charcas; but he was friendless, and they remained for three hours in a corner of the square, houseless and hungry. Miguel Cornejo saw them there when he went to church, and again when he came out; so he invited them into his house. Long afterwards, after Gonzalo had won the battle of Huarina, Carbajal marched to Arequipa. The citizens fled, but were overtaken and brought back by the followers of Carbajal, and among them was Miguel Cornejo. Old Carbajal sent for his former host, and told him that, for his sake, he would do no injury to the citizens or the town of Arequipa. When Giron rose in rebellion, Miguel Cornejo, with other citizens of Arequipa, joined the royal army under Pedro de Meneses. They were surprised by Giron at Villacuri, in the desert between Yca and Pisco, and retreated, making a running fight for three leagues. Cornejo wore a Burgundian helmet with a closed visor; and what with the heat and dust, he was suffocated, and so died, to the great sorrow of all who knew him; for he was a virtuous and generous knight.

[5] This was Francisco de Zarate, one of the three soldiers who were sent to Cuzco by Pizarro. See Note on p. 72. —

To Lozano	.	.	. 84...2220
To Garcia Lopez	.	.	. 135...3330
To Juan Muñoz	.	.	. 135...3330
To Juan de Berlanga ·	.	.	. 180...4440
To Esteban Garcia	.	.	. 94...4440
To Juan de Salvatierra	.	.	. 135...3330
To Pedro Calderon (*no gold*)	.	.	. 135... —
To Gaspar de Marquina (*no silver*)	.	.	. — ...3330
To Diego Escudero (*no silver*)	.	.	. — ...4440
To Cristobal de Sosa[6]	.	.	. 135...3330

The Governor also said that 20,000 *pesos* should be assigned to the men who came with the Captain Diego de Almagro, to aid them in paying their debts and freight, and to furnish them with some necessaries that they required.

He also said that 15,000 *pesos* of gold should be given to the thirty persons who remained in the city of San Miguel de Piura sick, and to others who were not present at the capture of the chief Atahuallpa nor at the taking of the gold; because some were poor and others had much need; and his Lordship ordered this sum to be distributed among those persons.

He also said that for the 8000 *pesos* which the company gave to Hernando Pizarro to enable him to explore the country, and for other things such as the work of the barber and surgeon, and for things that had been given the chiefs, 8000 *pesos* should be taken from the mass.

All which the Lord Governor declared to be good and to be well arranged, and he moreover declared that the sum which each man received might be taken by him in the name of God and his conscience, having respect to what his

---

[6] One of the assassins of Francisco Pizarro. See Note at p. 139.

Majesty had commanded; and he ordered that it should be given and distributed by weight, and before me, the notary, to each man as had been declared, signed by order of his Lordship.

PEDRO SANCHO.

THE END.

For EU product safety concerns, contact us at Calle de José Abascal, 56–1°, 28003 Madrid, Spain or eugpsr@cambridge.org.

www.ingramcontent.com/pod-product-compliance
Ingram Content Group UK Ltd.
Pitfield, Milton Keynes, MK11 3LW, UK
UKHW012341130625
459647UK00009B/446